**COLD CALLING**
**SIMPLE SYSTEMISED SUCCESS**

# KEVIN CHARLTON

First published in the United Kingdom in 2016
by Kevin Charlton.

ISBN: 978-1-326-64463-5

Cover design and interior formatting by ebook-designs.co.uk

# CONTENTS

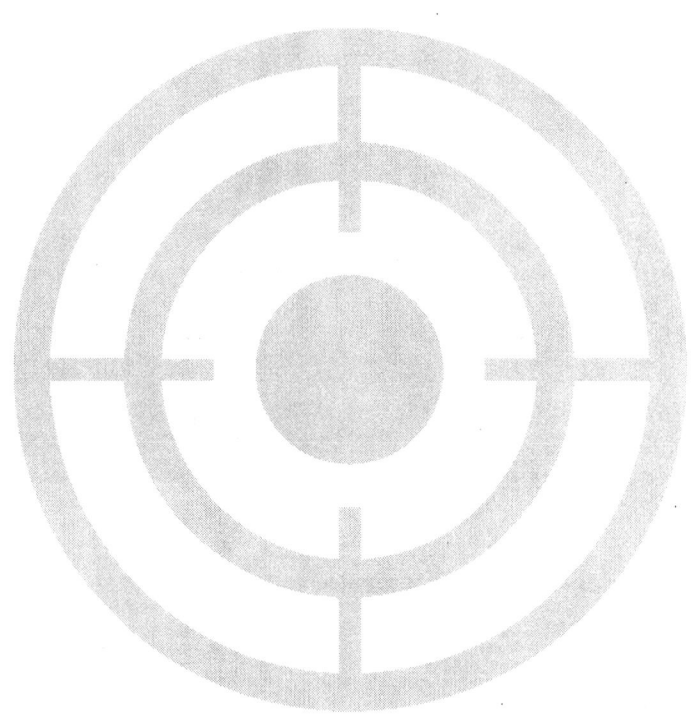

# ACKNOWLEDGEMENTS

It's done. My book, a lifetime in the making and a couple of years in production, has made it to print. There are a number of people who have encouraged me through this journey whom I would like to thank.

A good friend and a mentor of mine, Peter Thomson, convinced me that my experience and knowledge is valuable and should be shared with others. He gave me a structure to follow and the motivation to keep going when I wanted to stop.

George Mullen, my Father-in-Law, remains a huge inspiration to me. He demonstrated the real qualities required in running a business; belief in your ability; strength of character, determination, adaptability and how to react to setbacks.

I would like to thank my coaching clients who have successfully used these techniques and urged me to document them.

Most of all I want to thank my wife and three sons. They have always believed in what I do and have ensured more than anyone else I stuck to the task. Without them this book would not be written.

So Alison, Ed, Elliot, Harry and in memory of my gorgeous dog, Bunty who walked my thoughts with me, this is for you.

# PROLOGUE

**5:00 am July 6th. I climbed into my car to make the 200 mile journey to meet a potential new client at nine o'clock. I should be there early, which is my preference, but it was a Monday and the M6 is notoriously bad. I was cold; even in July the Sun hadn't yet flashed warmth onto the earth. I hadn't slept well, partly because my internal alarm clock kept jarring me awake, but mainly because I had to make "that" call. My Citroen Picasso wasn't the most glamorous of cars, but it was cheap to run and hadn't let me down; it grumbled into life and set off on a journey that it probably knew as well as I did.**

Have you ever had a life changing moment? One where you stood up for yourself and in a blaze of glory, committed to doing something completely different? I was a decent enough salesman and had sold a variety of products and services over the years and I had the title of National Sales Manager for a company providing training solutions. This meant I could travel anywhere in the Country to find my next client. I loved the idea of training and have always enjoyed the buzz of learning something new; so in that respect, this was a great job for me because I was passionate about what I was selling. Some of the trainers the company employed were really very good but others were, at best, average. But boy! Did they have a high opinion of themselves? Was it because they had developed an ego to match the title "Consultant" which appeared on their business cards?

I was not a trainer, but felt that I could be a good one. Communication was one of my strengths although there existed a mystique about what trainers did. They hid behind jargon, clever tests and exercises, to build the grandeur of their role.

As the salesman, my problem was that I had to justify the quality of the work we delivered to the clients and it was apparent that some clients were not happy with the standard of training they were receiving. My livelihood and that of my wife and three boys were dependent on my selling and retaining business. Training consultants commanded a much higher salary than I did, even though I had uncovered the client's problem and sold them a tailored solution. To compound matters I had agreed to move my family South, which meant my wife giving up her career and us having to settle the boys into new schools.

One of the senior trainers within the company seemed to be having a difference of opinion with the owners; it was bubbling under the surface and one evening, over a quiet drink, James asked me; *"How would you fancy going into business together? You're a good salesman and I'm a good trainer, I think we could do well"*

We discussed finding new clients and, in time, he would teach me what he knew so we could both deliver training. It appealed, but I was already struggling to pay the mortgage and credit card bills were mounting up. It was a huge risk with no guarantee of success. The idea was shelved; at least for that moment in time.

The Friday sales review came around and the owner of the business, normally charming and charismatic was ranting in the office and his focus of attention was on me. He was particularly upset because earlier in the day we had a good client tell us they were not renewing their contract and had chosen to go with a competitor.

*"It's simply not acceptable. I've got fourteen consultants to feed with work and some of them are only half utilised. Where's the extra work going to come from?"*

Like many people, I hate confrontation and especially when I'm being blamed for something outside my control. It was dark outside. The harsh strip lighting illuminated the sales whiteboards; they were a spider's web of coloured pen, numbers and dates, value of contracts and programmes yet to be started. My stomach was churning and I was trying to keep my composure as shouting back and arguing would resolve nothing.

*"I've been trying to tell you for months; we have several big accounts that should commence in the next quarter; but some clients are not renewing because the training team are not providing enough value"*

I could feel my rage rising; I had spent hours on the telephone generating fresh enquiries; driving 4000 miles per month to present ideas and solutions.

*"The problem with you is you're not getting in front of enough decision makers to hit target"*

It started to turn personal; he was questioning my commitment in the role and turning a blind eye to the deficiencies elsewhere.

*"We don't need fresh clients; we need to look after the ones we've got and if we were providing solutions to their problems, like we promised, they would be happy to spend more money with us!"*

*"Well as far as I'm concerned it's a numbers game and you're not seeing enough people and you've got a week to sort it out"* he barked.

That was the point that would change my life forever. He had got me to the tipping point. The pros and cons that had been bouncing around in my mind finally dropped one way. I stopped thinking of the consequences and very calmly and I hope with an air of professionalism, said:

*"Nick; I don't need another week to come up with a solution to your problem; I'm leaving right now"*

I turned on my heels and walked to the office door. Nick's tone changed as he insisted that I sit down. *"Come on, we can sort this out."* Was that slight desperation in his voice? *"Sorry Nick, best of luck!"*

A year on and I faced another big moment.
I had gone into business with James; it had been a tough start, but I proved that I really could sell and we picked up a number of new clients almost straight away. I felt inferior as the "salesman" and that James held all the magic. I was determined to learn more and enrolled on several courses and workshops. I enlisted on the Tony Robbins "Unleash the Power Within" seminar and walked on hot coals; I invested in books and audio tapes so I could continue my education whilst driving around the Country.

It became apparent that James had very limited training knowledge and like all other consultants from the previous company, was happy to regurgitate the same old training techniques. What's more he had very different values to me and wanted a different lifestyle from the company. I was the one driving the business forwards both literally and metaphorically and James wasn't putting in the hours or the labour but still taking 50% of the profit. In short, I was carrying a passenger. From his perspective he felt that he still held the ace cards. After all he was the trainer!

At home; we had been discussing the situation quietly for a few weeks.

*"You can't keep on this way". "You are all over the place selling and making promises and James is undermining you because he's not prepared to change his training methods or adapt"*

But deep down I was afraid that I would be found wanting when it came to training and coaching. I became snappy and irritable. It was the fear of the unknown and my limiting beliefs, holding me back. But today I would face the fear!

In my mind we could simply divide up our clients and provided they were agreeable, we would continue to work with them individually. I even thought through the consequences and planned to give James the lion's share to make the decision more palatable. I hadn't told anyone that I would do it today.

At 5:15 am and finally on the M6 I made the call. I knew James would still be in bed and the call would probably go to answer-phone. Maybe this was the coward's way out but I wanted him to have time to digest the message before calling me back.

*"Hi James, it's me. Give me a call when you pick up; we need to have a chat. This isn't working for me and I think we need to go our separate ways"*

That was it. No going back now; for the second time in just over a year I'd made a decision that would take me completely out of my comfort zone.

James called back about 6:30 and he was calm; perhaps almost smug. When I suggested on the split of clients he no doubt felt he had the upper hand and all was agreed amicably.

What I wasn't expecting was the wave of relief that poured over me. Yes I'd made a massive decision, but instead of being worried I felt excited about the future. What was the worst that could happen? I could fail, but all of the decisions were in my hands.

I learned very quickly that training isn't complicated. It's about understanding individual problems and helping people to develop. Fast forward more than a decade and I still have clients that I started with on day one. I gain most of my business through referrals and I work with clients across the whole of the UK helping them develop people in their organisations and make more money. Without mystique!

> **"I learned very quickly that training isn't complicated. It's about understanding individual problems and helping people to develop."**

There is one skill that I have honed over the years, (initially as a necessity for my business to survive) One which is essential for every entrepreneur or salesperson. Without this, even with the best products and services in the world, your business will suffer. The purpose of this book is to share with you my ideas so you can follow a **SYSTEM** to make you more successful in this one area.

(Oh yes! James is now a manager in someone else's business!)

# INTRODUCTION

My left hand was trembling as I moved my coffee cup slightly to the left of the desk; my pens were already organised in parallel, straight as soldiers, adjacent to the diary with its gleaming white page unspoiled by ink. The last number was pressed but connection not yet made; why was my mouth so dry? Random thoughts bounced around in my head. Must concentrate. Stick to the script and don't sound nervous; keep control. I wonder who'll answer? They'll no doubt be superefficient and practised at dismissing the call. I hope they're in a good mood. It's easy for them; it's not their mortgage and bills at stake. Maybe they won't answer and, even if they do, I probably won't get to speak to the person in charge. So that's ok, I can call another time. Should I have sent a letter first and then called? Would that have been more professional? I don't want to look unprofessional! Whoa I feel sick!

Of course it's irrational. I always knew I was a great communicator, everyone told me so. It was easy for me to make friends and building rapport at any level just came naturally to me. Why then, when it came to picking up the telephone, did my natural talents ebb away from me..."It's only a piece of plastic".

I know I'm not alone. Almost every salesperson I talk to has the same fears. They may have a fantastic offer, product or service and when they are able to sit in front of the right decision-maker they can be very convincing; but making the initial call to get there proves a massive challenge.

I've worked in sales all my life and I really enjoy it. There's a buzz from knowing you've helped someone and they are happy to buy from you. It's unlike any other feeling and when they purchase time after time and refer others to you; it almost instills a new line of code into your DNA. A satisfaction that you are a competent professional, respected in your field of expertise and safe in the knowledge that you no longer fall into the perceived category of an unscrupulous purveyor of goods and chattels.

> **"I've worked in sales all my life and I really enjoy it. There's a buzz from knowing you've helped someone and they are happy to buy from you."**

But let's be honest, it's also a tough role. Your income and livelihood are dependent on your ability to get in front of people who share an interest in what you have to offer. Then your talent and skills to communicate the same and persuade your potential customer to part with money come into play. The range and scope of sales professionals are endless. Negotiating multi-billion pound defence projects involving capital expenditure, selling insurance products, promoting the latest IT software programmes; contract cleaning services; selling widgets and screws...there is no end!

I don't think I will ever forget the nauseous feeling of those early days. I vividly recall selling life assurance on a commission only basis. My leads had to be self-generated. I would work on trade stands, cold call local businesses, literally knocking door to door, all with the aim of getting the name of a decision maker so I could call them by telephone to gain an appointment, not even knowing at that stage whether they had any interest in what I had to offer. I was quite young and inexperienced. I had one young son and another on the way and the pressure to be successful was immense. How could I fail? How would I explain to my children that we couldn't afford the presents they wanted for Christmas or tell them why we wouldn't be going on holiday like their friends. Consequently I stuck at it, whilst others failed and left. Did I get better? Yes. But only when I started to learn from my mistakes and teach myself methods that would make the calls easier. My number one objective was to make comfortable calls and not to feel the negativity or rejection which lay at the heart of my fear.

With the wisdom of years and the skills gained in a variety of sales roles I developed a **SYSTEM** for making successful calls based upon my own experience. For twenty years now I've been training and coaching others to be successful in sales and a large portion of what I teach is about lead generation and giving people confidence to pick up the telephone. A few years ago I read a great book by Simon Sinek entitled *"Start with Why"* I would whole heartedly recommend this book because it drastically changed my thinking. Simon talks about really successful businesses and leaders in those organisations and he points out that it doesn't matter **what** you do, it matters **why** you do it.

I started thinking about my "WHY." It turns out, what I'm really passionate about, is helping others to achieve greatness. In sales, so many people are held back because of their inability to get the best out of telephone calling, so I decided to teach my **SYSTEM** to others to see what a real difference it can make to their lives. At the time of writing this book I have coached salespeople to make more than 14,000 sales appointments; so I know it works.

In order to get my methods out to a greater audience I have compiled this book so you too can have the template for success; a blueprint to create any outbound call and to massively increase your chances of success. Calls are structured around what I call the "**5 P's of Telephone Success"** and as you read through each chapter I will guide you to create your own call format and to learn techniques to overcome objections.

Imagine what a difference this could make to your confidence and results. If you were able to double the number of appointments gained from half the effort and number of calls; how much of a financial and emotional difference would that make to your life?

I know it's made a massive difference to many of my clients. So thank you for investing in this book and let me repay you by giving you the secrets to my **5-Step System** called **It's Your Call** "*Cold Calling – Simple Systemised Success*" so you can generate more appointments, make more sales and earn more money.

# Chapter One: Preparation

The first of the 5 P's is preparation and it is without doubt, the most important because lack of adequate preparation, predisposes failure.

So, let's go back to **WHY!**

Traditional business models have generally followed the model below. This is what we do; this is how we go about it which makes us better than anyone else, so this is why you should buy from us.

## **WHAT** ........ HOW ........ WHY

As previously discussed, Simon Sinek explains eloquently ***"People don't buy what you do...they buy why you do it"***

Simon uses the example of Apple Inc. to demonstrate the point and how from the top down it was the communication of why they did things, not what they did that has made them so successful. Even today they remain market leaders because of their ability to give clarity to their WHY. The technology and creative ideas were not necessarily founded by Apple. Creative Technology Ltd; a Singapore -based company created the technology for mp3 players, which would transform the way in which we consume music and completely change the model in this industry. The problem for Creative technology was they described their product as a "5GB mp3 player". It is exactly the same message as Apple's "1,000 songs in your pocket". The difference is Creative told us **WHAT** their product was and Apple told us **WHY** we needed it.

I was guilty of following the traditional model when starting my business and I think many others do the same thing. My message was; this is my training company, it's clean fresh and innovative; this is what I do that makes me different from all the competition; I think we can work well together and I can make you more money...hire me.

Don't get me wrong, you need to have good products and you do need to demonstrate tangible differentiation, but without the magic ingredient of WHY you are doing it the message can be easily copied by the next budding training consultant. In my formative years of business I concentrated on creating new products and training ideas that would make my clients do things in a different way and produce them greater results and it worked. But for every great idea I came up with, there was a copycat version on the market shortly afterwards and clients would make a decision on how well a company promoted itself or on price.

I am very successful and benefit from extremely loyal clients who provide me with lots of referrals. When I started to consider my WHY I discovered that whilst my ideas and methods were important; the real reason people bought my training was because of my passion for helping individuals within the organisations to develop. Companies are simply a collection of people and my focus has always been on coaching individuals.

As I made each person more successful, many of them have moved onto very senior positions and still call upon me to help develop the skills of their teams and are delighted to recommend me further. Unbeknown to me at the time, I had triggered a chemical reaction in the people I had helped, which is called the process of **reciprocity.** In social psychology it refers to a positive action being rewarded by another positive action. As a social construct, reciprocity means that in response to friendly actions, people are frequently much nicer and much more cooperative than predicted by the self-interest model. Conversely, in response to hostile actions they are frequently much nastier and even brutal. In other words, because I had helped them become more successful they almost feel obliged to help me become more successful in return, by speaking highly of me and referring me on. Of course with this model I'm limited to the number of people I can help, hence the reason for this book so I can share ideas with a wider audience.

You need to take time to think about your WHY.

# **WHY** ........ HOW ........ WHAT

When you learn how to communicate the reason you are in business, or the real WHY behind the organisation you represent; you'll find a real passion and belief which will have a dramatic impact on your delivery of the message. Later in this book we will examine exactly how you will formulate your message in a concise way so the listener and your prospective customer can justify reasons to engage with you.

## **Understanding & Encoding of Information**

Many years ago I was working with managers who sold Honda Cars and they were excitedly explaining to me that for an extra £10 per month; they could get me out of my existing petrol Honda Civic and provide me with a brand new Honda Civic Diesel (their latest car to come to market at the time).I asked them how well the promotion was going and how eager their customers were to buy, to which I received a mixed response; *"some are buying...others are not."*

To explain why, on the face of it, a relatively strong offer was not working; I told them about how humans make decisions and explained the pitfalls of their approach.  Scientists estimate that humans first existed on earth 6-7 million years ago. The environment at the time was very different from today. In order to survive, we have the 'fight or flight' reflex.

You have probably heard of this, but for completeness here is my very basic understanding.

When we are afraid of something, the hypothalamus in the brain activates the sympathetic nervous system and the adrenal- cortex. The sympathetic nervous system uses the nerves to trigger responses whilst the adrenal cortex uses the blood. When the hypothalamus is stimulated by fear, it basically tells the body either to stay and fight, run away, or stand perfectly still (freeze) so that it is not detected by the predator!  Whichever reaction the body adopts, adaptations must be made to facilitate this. Initially the heart speeds up to deliver more oxygen around the body. The adrenal cortex releases adrenaline, which together with the sympathetic system cause changes in the physical state. The pupils in the eyes dilate to take in more light. Blood is diverted to the major muscle groups in the legs and feet to enable running or to the arms and hands for fighting. More oxygen is allowed into the lungs whilst the digestive system decreases its activity. The brain is unable to focus on complex tasks, only considering the escape route and survival.

Imagine a caveman faced with a wild animal charging towards him. His instinct would be either to stand there and fight it and probably eat it; or to run away and seek safety in the woods or cave.

We all experience the same thing on a regular basis. Growing up through our school days we may have been cornered by the school bully and we immediately made a decision to fight him/her or run away. Faced with a bus hurtling towards us as we cross a busy street, the adrenalin kicks in enable us to run away and survive.

All of this happens in an instant which is why it is called a reflex. As it is a primitive response, it has been aptly name 'crocodile brain' by Oren Klaff in his book "Pitch Anything".

This primeval crocodile brain served the human race well. As we evolved the crocodile brain was surrounded by the mid-brain, which puts everything into a social context. We like to live in families and have people around us. For anyone reading with medical knowledge, please excuse me for over simplifying the workings of the human brain as I do so simply to make a point.

The outside portion of the brain is called the neocortex and is generally regarded as the thinking part of the brain where we make rational decisions, compute the information and make judgments.

A very close bedfellow to fear is anxiety which is more often the trigger for us today.

To put this into context. Imagine you are walking home on a dark night and you are about to put the key into your front door and go into the warmth and light. Just as you are about to do this, someone shouts loudly behind you. Your instinctive reaction will be to jump as your crocodile brain leaps into action; you turn to see if it has anything to do with you (mid-brain) and then quickly work out (neocortex) that it is someone shouting to another person further up the street.

What this tells us is the encoding of information starts at the crocodile brain and if it feels it is necessary to pass it on, the message will travel through the mid brain to the neocortex so it can process it and decide what actions to take. Naturally this happens in fractions of seconds with electrical impulses. The crocodile brain is lazy and if it has no interest in the information it won't bother starting the process of understanding.

So how does this relate to our Honda managers? When pitching an offer (For an extra £10 per month.....) they are appealing to the neocortex. Whilst some people will see this as a positive offer and quickly react in the affirmative; many more will decipher the information as making a change and immediately go into fear mode (effectively wanting to run away). So not only do they respond in a negative way, their brain immediately starts to justify why they shouldn't buy the new car, formulating reasons to stick with their existing car and maintain status-quo. So the thoughts are probably along the lines of: *"No I like my existing car" "It's a really nice colour and low mileage" "I don't see any need to change"* and so on. I suggested to the team that they should perhaps change their approach and consider the consequences of the customer not changing the car. To this end we made a list of the hidden expenses of keeping their existing car or the potential missed savings of changing. The list was extensive including; losing out on a remarkable fuel saving each year; the fact that they would have to pay for road tax and breakdown recovery, which they were probably paying for separately. The cost of servicing was built in with the cost of the new car along with other discounts they hadn't considered; and of course there were no impending maintenance costs.

Changing the approach meant that they could provide the customer with massive benefits to change before positioning the fact that, to do so, would also mean very little additional capital outlay at £10 per month.

The 'away' motivated approach is often more powerful (The consequence of doing nothing as opposed to making a change for change sake) than the towards motivation. The results were dramatically different and positive for all concerned.

This is a valuable point to consider when creating any sales pitch or constructing your telephone approach. In many instances the person you are calling will have no idea who you are, what you are offering or how it will benefit them. I mentioned earlier that in sales all you do is provide solutions to problems. If the solutions are a good fit for the problem; there's a possibility that you may make a sale. However, before you provide the solution you need to be able to highlight the problem the customer may not know they've got. In effect you need to be able to demonstrate very quickly the "before and after" scenarios.

## The Motivation to Buy

Now that we have a basic understanding of the physiology of the brain, it is worth considering the factors influencing our decisions to change something; to buy, or at least to consider investigating the possibility of doing something different. I would like to introduce you to my **B.E.V.A.** principle; a technique to help people fully prepare before making a presentation of a product or service or indeed before they pick up the telephone to make an appointment.

The acronym stands for **B**enefit –**E**motion-**V**alue- **A**sk

Forgive me for starting with something quite basic for people in sales; but you'd be surprised how simple it is to make a mistake with this part. We all know that people must understand the benefits of your product or service in order to work out whether it will be useful to them, or not. All too frequently, salespeople or business owners slip back into presenting the features of their product.

I'm sure you hear examples of it every day but this is a real conversation that happened to me recently when I was attempting to book my car in for a routine service. After getting through the initial pleasantries and data capture for my vehicle this is how the call proceeded:

| | |
|---|---|
| Advisor: | *"The car is due a full scheduled service; or would you like us to carry out another interim one as we did last time?* |
| Me: | *"I'm not sure, what's the difference?"* |
| Advisor: | *"OK with the scheduled service you get spark plugs, oil filter and pollen filter"* |
| Me: | *"And how much more does it cost?* |
| Advisor: | *"£80"* |
| Me: | *"I'll have the interim one please"* |

The problem with this conversation is the advisor has simply provided me with features of what the service includes and not the benefits to me. Because my knowledge of cars is extremely limited, I can only consider the extra parts I'm being offered and the additional cost, before making my decision. On the other hand, consider how my decision may have changed if I was given the following explanation to my questions:

*Advisor:*

*"OK with a scheduled service we fit new spark plugs so your car remains reliable and will start every morning. We change*

*the pollen filter to ensure the air you breathe inside the car is clean and fresh, so if you suffer with allergies it will keep you more comfortable and healthy. We also change the oil filter on the car, which helps to prolong the life of the engine; it helps towards improving miles per gallon and lessens the chance of needing expensive maintenance in the future, which will save you money. The additional cost is only £80 and is recommended; shall we go ahead?"*

This time I can associate the real benefits with the additional cost and make an informed decision. It is so easy for all of us to slip into jargon and to assume the customer understands and has the background knowledge that we take for granted. So for clarity; a feature is what the product or service has (5GB Mp3 player) the benefit is what it will do for me, the customer (1000 songs in your pocket). Remember to check your presentations or calls so the customer can easily identify the benefits.

> **"It is so easy for all of us to slip into jargon and to assume the customer understands and has the background knowledge that we take for granted."**

When we buy anything, we do so for an emotional reason hence the **E** in BEVA.

Children are very persuasive when they want an ice cream, even though it's not healthy for them we often end up buying them one, either to make them smile or to pacify a situation. When those same children reach adolescence we can find ourselves spending an additional £20 or more to buy the trainers they "really want". We do so of course, because we love them and don't want them to feel out of place with their friends. Whilst the cost is higher than expected, we make the purchase because it makes us feel good about our ability to make them happy and in doing so, it positively affects our self-esteem.

I'm sure you can recall many times when you've spent a little extra when buying clothes or shoes; justifying the purchase because they make you feel a little better or because the brand is a little more exclusive?

A big decision often takes more thought but the motivations are the same. If you are to buy a new house, it is a big decision and you'll have completed plenty of homework before collecting the keys from the estate agent. You'll have thought about location; specification; local amenities; insurance additional expenditure and so on. The real decision however, happens in a heartbeat! When you open the door into the house and its everything you expected and more your emotions will be raised. On the other hand if it disappoints on room size or decor, the emotion slips back.

It's the emotion that triggers the next action. If I'm excited or motivated, then I will make the next step in the process (put an offer in on the house). If I'm less motivated, procrastination kicks in and we tend to want to "think about it." Of course emotions will depend on the product or service being offered and the problem it may solve. If I'm buying a new TV or car the emotions will often be excitement; status; pride and so forth. When I'm considering buying life assurance or fixing the brakes on my car; the emotions are more likely to be safety; legality; peace of mind. It doesn't matter what the emotions are; unless they are triggered by your presentation; the customer will hold back.

The next part of B.E.V.A. is VALUE. Consider for a moment the difference between price and value. Imagine you see a cut crystal ornament in a department store in the high street with a price tag of £20.

The same ornament (undamaged) is now on sale in the local village fair or boot sale; what do you think the price may be now? (£2-£3?)

Now imagine the same ornament on sale in the West End of London in Harrods shop window; proudly standing on a thick blue velvet cushion and displayed under lights so it glistens and shimmers to all who pass by. Now what do you think the price tag may be? (£200-£300?)

You see, price is simply a number whereas value is perception! Of course we all have a different value set; for example a good friend of mine will pay £100 for a tie! I think he's a bit crazy because I would never spend so much on something which can be so easily damaged or spoiled. But he likes them; sometimes they are limited edition ties and it makes him feel special. If a management consultant charged £10,000 per day for their services, you may consider that to be expensive; however, if after immediately using him and adopting the changes he suggested, your company made an additional £1,000,000 in profit; then presumably, like me, you would think it was money well spent and good value.

This brings us to another very important point, which I call the "Contrast Principle" Whether you like it or not, we all position things in our head and unconsciously start to contrast the situation with what we think fits our value set.

Twenty five years after buying bedroom furniture from a reputable department store, Fenwick of Newcastle and having moved house several times, it was fair to say that the furniture was starting to look a little shabby. The purchase price was quite high at £1600 and as a struggling young married couple we paid on credit and lovingly looked after it. The quality had been excellent and years later when we finally decided to refit our bedroom we were able to sell the wardrobes on the Internet for £200, so all in all, very satisfactory.

When deciding on replacement furniture it was natural for us to consider the same manufacturer, even though it was likely to be expensive.

The representative turned up at the appointed time dressed very professionally in a dark suit and carrying a very heavy case of sample drawer fronts. He spent the first twenty five minutes building rapport, explaining the company history and generally building value in dealing with a reputable organisation with over 60 years' experience. (The price was going to be high!).

He complimented us on our bedroom layout and proceeded to take meticulous measurements in order to create a 3D diagram on his laptop. Two hours later, when I was starting to lose the will to live, he sat forward on the sofa preparing to give us the bad news.

I could see this beautiful image of our bedroom on his laptop and had to agree with him that it appeared a worthy replacement. Of course I had a figure in mind, it must be £7,000 - £8,000? I hoped it wasn't going to be more than that.

*"For all of this beautiful furniture, fitted by our in-house craftsmen and with the 10 year guarantee, the cost will be £3,900"*

There was a pause as he looked first at my wife and then to me for a reaction. Not wanting to sound too eager we excused ourselves to another room and in whispered voice and wide eyed conversation, we congratulated ourselves on making an outstanding decision. Surely he had made a mistake? He must have missed something off the quote.

Filled with optimism and still wanting to get a "deal" I regained my composure to negotiate. After a bit of haggling he agreed an overall price of £3,150 at which point I signed an order and gave a deposit. I had a signed order in my hand so there would be no going back now.

The order was correct, the craftsmen were as good as described and the finished bedroom exceeded our expectations. I'm sure that I could have got a cheaper bedroom from a competitor, but my contrast was with the price twenty five years ago and frankly I thought I received outstanding value.

Imagine you're running a sale weekend (the product doesn't matter) and you position your offer like this:

Price was:    £2,500
Price now:   £2,000
Save:          £500

As the customer, seeing this pricing technique; what is the first thing you would ask for? If you're like me, you'd probably ask for more discount, because if you can give me £500 immediately how much more can you give me? In my opinion; you are sometimes better off simply stating it as *Event Price... this weekend only £2,000.* At least it would then be necessary to discuss with the sales team how it represents value. Remember, some people will also consider your price to be too cheap and therefore discount your ability to perform. This is how luxury and premium goods are sold because their status is something customers are buying into and to be given a discounted price may offend, and it seemingly devalues the brand.

The final part of any presentation, and the "A" in BEVA, is to ASK for the business; the appointment or the next action. It's surprising how many people struggle with this part of the process and looking back, to my early years in sales, I wasn't very good because I wasn't trained to ask. I learned bad techniques from work colleagues which more often than not, did not commit the other person to making a decision. Of course it was more comfortable because I rarely received a direct "no" as an answer. Instead I collected a lot of "maybes". There are lots of ways to ask; a direct close (shall we go ahead?) An alternative close (do you want the red one or blue one?) An assumptive close (all I need is your credit card) A conditional close (if I can... will you...) A summary close (so you want "X" along with "Y" and you said you must have "Z"...I think that's everything...sign here) There's even something called a 'puppy dog close'!

The puppy dog close is about removing the risk. Imagine going into a pet shop with your children who are excitedly playing with the adorable puppies. The pet shop owner; realising you are in doubt about this long-term commitment; gives you the killer line in front of your children: *"I know it's a big decision so why not take the dog home for the night and if you are still undecided in the morning; just bring him back"* Guess how many puppies are returned?

The same principle is used routinely on the Internet, when you are considering purchasing a set of diet or fitness CD's. At the end of the sales pitch they explain there is a 100% money-back guarantee...if you are not happy simply return the CD's in the original packaging up to 30 days later. This helps us make the initial decision and the incidence of returns is minimal.

When I fail to sell my product or service I now take a step back to re-examine my approach to find out which part of BEVA was missing or weak. Almost always I find that it is the emotion or value that are lacking.

## Communication and Persuasion

In order to persuade others to do as we want, we must first examine how we communicate with one another and how we develop sufficient rapport so they may choose our course of action. The Oxford English dictionary definition of rapport is *"Relationship"* which is quite a broad term and doesn't adequately describe the process we go through to create the state of rapport. Many would say it's being on the same wavelength as another or finding common ground.

As you probably realise, the process of building rapport starts some time before we start talking to the other person and finding possible common ground. In fact when I first saw the model of communication (face to face); I was surprised. This model includes three elements; the words we use; the way in which we deliver those words and body language.

| | |
|---|---|
| **Words** | **7%** |
| **Voice Quality** | **38%** |
| **Body Language** | **55%** |

I consider myself to be a very good communicator... and I love to talk!

After due consideration and thinking about my children growing up; I realised that a lot of my communication was body language. With my children taking their first steps, for example, I would clap my hands and smile, rather than use words.

Non-verbal communication includes, posture and gestures,(the nod of a head, the movement of our hands and so forth). It includes facial feedback, eye contact; your proximity to others and how tactile you are; it even includes the pace of your breathing and blinking.

It only takes a matter of seconds for us to pick up on these non-verbal clues and to make decisions on others. Have you ever experienced walking into a shop heading towards a sales assistant for help; only to have a change of heart about that person and to turn away in favour of another assistant? I know I have. It can be something as simple as the way they looked at you or your interpretation of their attitude based on their posture. It's chemistry between people at an unconscious level which allows us to decide if we are comfortable with one another. It also allows us to strike up relationships with our partners; words don't have to pass lips for you both to know.

The science of rapport building has been superbly explored by John Grinder and Richard Bandler. They co-edited a number of books on NLP (Neuro Linguistic Programming) in which they discuss "Modelling" other's actions to improve levels of rapport. Following in the footsteps of Milton Ericson; they were the first to identify the "Mirroring & Matching" technique to enable people to build effective rapport.

In everyday circumstances, we adopt these techniques without thought. Spend enough time with someone and you'll find that you are instinctively copying their language patterns or actions. When they lean in to talk to you; you do the same; if they relax and sit back in a chair you often find you are also adopting a more relaxed position.

Grinder and Bandler perfected the techniques and taught them to others so they had the ability to increase powers of persuasion or to change the state of an individual to adopt different programmes. These techniques are regularly used to assist with dieting; giving up smoking; fear of flying etc. Programmes are simply the habits we have adopted. Every morning I start my shaving programme at the same point on my face. My tie is routinely knotted in the same way that my father showed me decades ago. (Have you ever tried putting a tie on someone else...it's hard!) Driving to work is effortless; I don't consider the number of gear changes but stop instantly at every red light. The Army trains techniques so cadets can strip a rifle and put it together again in seconds; they call it muscle memory. The same techniques become habits. With piano practice, eventually, the pianist does not need to read the music, but follow the trained techniques they have practiced for hours.

In addition to the physical modeling; Grinder and Bandler focus on the importance of language patterns and how a simple change of phrase or wording in a sentence can be encoded in a very different way; therefore changing the outcome. This is a vital point in the construction of your sales pitch which we will uncover shortly.

Most salespeople are comfortable in dealing with people face to face; but when it comes to the telephone, the visual clues are removed and many of us find it difficult to compensate. We will discuss this in chapter three and how to maximise your chances of building rapport over the telephone.

# Different Strokes for Different Folks

Life would be really boring if everyone was the same and one of the great pleasures of working in a sales environment, is you get to meet so many different personalities. It's inevitable that we are going to get on with some people better than others and when it comes to selling you need to be adaptable. In the past, I wondered why I was brilliant at selling certain products some months and in the following month, completely the opposite. The products hadn't changed; nor had the price or my presentation style. But, I was failing to adapt to the different customer personalities presented to me.

There are four basic personality styles dictated by their level of assertiveness and their responsiveness towards other people.

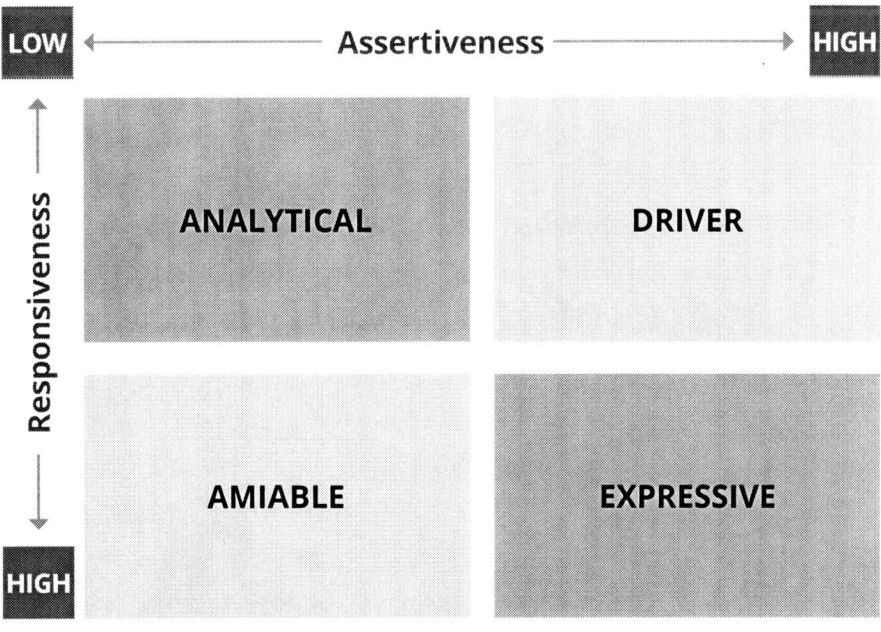

**Driver**

Driver personality types are very easy to spot, even before they begin to speak. They tend to walk tall; move at pace; make strong eye contact and give very little facial feedback. When they do talk they will be quite forthright and factual; they will talk louder than most and they have no idle time for social "chit chat". They are task orientated people, who demand attention and make quick decisions. They are naturally assertive by nature, they enjoy competition and winning and they will not care particularly about the feelings of others in achieving their tasks. The way in which they dress is no guide to their personality type; they may be a "power dresser" but equally may be wearing overalls and wellington boots; it's the personality traits you have to watch out for.

This is a little more challenging to spot when they are on the telephone and you don't have the benefit of visual clues. Nevertheless, you will hear a confident tone and an assured approach; they will get to the point and you will be left in no doubt about what they want to achieve from the conversation. They are impatient and will pick up on any doubt in your voice and question any lack of clarity in your reply.

So what is the best way to deal with this personality type? Well I like to think of them as the "School Bully"; parading around, demanding to be centre of attention; boosting their ego and status by picking on less dominant types with a view to building their personal entourage. You have to stand up to a "bully" to gain the respect you deserve. Now this is quite difficult for many people but it is a skill that can be learned. You need to be factual and to the point with a "driver" and back up your conversation with reasoned arguments. They like a challenge but will respect you more when they hear the word "No".

To illustrate the point, here is a typical car dealership inbound telephone call where a customer is calling about a specific car they have seen advertised:

Salesperson: *"Hello you are through to John Smith in sales, how can I help you?"*

"Driver" Customer: *"I'm interested in the 64 plate black Vauxhall Astra on your web site. What's the best deal you can do on that?"*

You will note that the caller does not use the name of the salesperson; they are abrupt and straight to the point. They are confident they will achieve a good deal and this is reflected in their voice which is loud and full of authority.

Salesperson: *"Yes I know the one, it's an outstanding vehicle it has only just arrived and we've had a number of calls since we put it on the website."*

*"Can you tell me is it just that particular vehicle or one in that price range that is of interest"*

The salesperson has recognised the style of the customer from the voice quality and understands that this "Driver" personality must be confronted in a professional way because the "Driver" will respect this approach. The salesperson has indicated that it is a popular car therefore limiting the expectations of the caller to expect to any discount. By seeking further information, the salesperson is taking control. He's attempting to establish if this is a unique car to the caller in which case price may not be paramount to the decision.

----------------------------------------------------------

"Driver" Customer: *"No just that car. So what's the best deal?"*

They have returned to the very direct and demanding question style typical of the driver but the caller has now conceded slightly and probably lowered his chances of gaining a significant discount. This is because the salesperson is now aware that as no other car is of interest, they probably have a unique offering.

Salesperson: *"The car has been priced competitively to sell, but tell me do you have a car to part exchange against it?"*

Again the salesperson is defending the price and standing up to the "Bully" personality and continuing to open up the conversation.

---

"Driver" Customer: *"Possibly. I have a 3 year old Ford Focus, but I just want to know what sort of deal you can do."*

The "Driver" is grudgingly handing over information but may now be losing patience. The salesperson recognises this and quickly responds.

---

Salesperson: *"We always do great deals. As I say the car is competitively priced, but I'm sure we can work something out. You need to come and see the car to fully appreciate it and of course we need to see your current car; so can you make it down later this afternoon or in the morning?*

When selling to a "Driver" personality they will appreciate a robust defence but the salesperson is now allowing the customer to hear a little submissiveness. In doing so the "Driver" will feel back in control. They will not want to lose out on the car and will likely agree to the appointment.

------------------------------------------------------------

## Amiable

As you can see from the diagram above, the amiable characters are almost the opposites of the driver. They are not assertive but very responsive towards other people. Again they are easily spotted, quite often in couples or pairs; they walk slightly round shouldered with a lack of pace and in a timid manner. They make poor eye contact but do give warm facial feedback. They don't make quick decisions and will avoid risks at all costs. When you engage them in conversation they are avid listeners and appear quite easily persuaded by your conversation. They want to remain friendly at all times and are keen not to upset anyone. Some may see this type of personality as an easy target; someone they can manipulate. This may be true; but not until time has been spent earning their trust and making them feel at ease.

Over the telephone, their voice will be weak. They are polite, so they won't interrupt you or give very much feedback other than tentative agreements. Their language will not be forceful; they will use sentences with soft edges (perhaps; maybe; possible; could etc.) They'll take a while to get to the point and even when they do it still may be unclear what they actually want to achieve from the conversation.

Dealing with amiable personalities takes time and patience. They do not like to be rushed and will not make quick decisions, in spite of the best efforts of many salespeople. Reassurance is important and they are happy to follow the crowd. Therefore the salesperson needs to adopt phrases like; "Most customers are doing it this way because..."

Using the same inbound call scenario as we did previously, we will identify the change in approach:

Salesperson: *"Hello you are through to John Smith in sales, how can I help you?"*

--------------------------------------------------------

"Amiable" Customer: *"Hello John, I wonder if you can help me. I've noticed you have a black Vauxhall Astra on your website can you tell me a little more about it"*

The customer acknowledges and uses the name of the salesperson because it is the polite thing to do. The language they use is not demanding and they don't give clear direction on what they want from the conversation.

--------------------------------------------------------

Salesperson: *"Yes I know the one, it's a lovely car it's only just come in and has only had one previous owner and they've really looked after it. We've had a number of calls since we put it on the website so it is very popular."*

*"Can you tell me is it just that particular vehicle or one in that price range that is of interest"*

The salesperson will recognise the almost timid and apologetic voice quality and should match that with soft and re-assuring language. Giving the "Amiable" a story in the life of the car will build desire. Once again the salesperson will need to identify if it is a unique opportunity with the follow up question.

"Amiable" Customer: *"No it's just that black one I want, it looks lovely."*

The caller has now admitted their desire for that particular car but probably still need convincing further before making any sort of commitment.

Salesperson: *"I think you are making a wise choice; tell me what do you use the car for and what are you currently driving?*

Re-assuring the "Amiable" customer that they are making a wise decision is paramount. The salesperson recognises the need to make friends with the customer and by asking open questions they will acknowledge their interest in the friendship.

---

"Amiable" Customer: ***"Well we have a three year old Ford Focus. We only really do local shopping and occasionally visit the grandchildren up North."***

The "Amiable" will be delighted to share personal stories. They want to make friends and trust the salesperson and they are in no hurry to make decisions. The salesperson must continue the dialog and not hurry the conversation.

---

*"That's nice. How old are your grandchildren and when you say up North, where do you mean exactly?"*

Taking the conversation away from the car and any "deal" will work well with the "Amiable" customer. They will feel relaxed and under no pressure. They often need guiding to the next stage.

*"Now I take it you will want to part exchange your Ford Focus and we would love to see it. As I said this particular car is clearly popular and I would hate for you to miss out. So can you come down*

*later on this afternoon or in the morning to see if you like it?"*

The salesperson has the interests of the "Amiable" at heart and is taking control of the next stage in the process.

----

## EXPRESSIVE

The character is in the title. Expressive people are quite assertive and persuasive. They care about what others think of them and enjoy working as part of a team. Expressive people are very sociable; they are comfortable and enjoy being the centre of attention. They are generous with facial feedback, make strong eye contact and gesture a lot with their hands. Mostly, they are predisposed to visual representations; responding well to pictures and stories and using visual language in everyday conversations for example: see; imagine; watch; picture; etc. The have large egos.

During conversation, expressive people show a genuine interest in making friends and as such will talk about the weather, holidays, sports, families and so on. They thrive on social engagement and will happily deal with you, even at a higher price; if they feel respected and comfortable.

On the telephone they can appear very friendly, picking up on jokes and responding well to conversations. They are good listeners but have a very short attention span (they want to get back to talking about them) so you must keep the interest levels high. The tone and inflection is upbeat and generally they will not want to upset you, so they may make promises in order to let you down gently at a later stage.

Expressive personalities are often the easiest to sell to, provided you make friends. They don't want to let you down and will often deal with you at the expense of others because of such implied loyalty.

So with our call scenario the "Expressive" personality could be handled in this way:

Salesperson: *"Hello you are through to John Smith in sales, how can I help you?"*

---

"Expressive" Customer: *"Hi John, You know that black Vauxhall Astra you have on your web site; the 64 plate with the blacked out windows. Can you see what sort of deal you can do for me on that?"*

The customer is more informal in using the salespersons name. The "Expressive" will utilise descriptive language and use visual connotations. The will talk in an upbeat optimistic way hoping for a deal rather than demanding one.

Salesperson: *"Yes I know the one, it's a looks fantastic. We've had a number of calls since we put it on the website. It's a very attractive car."*

*"Can you tell me is it just that particular vehicle or one in that price range that is of interest"*

The salesperson has picked up on the friendly tone and recognised the visual language patterns. In agreeing with the customer that it looks fantastic it will brush their ego. Once again the salesperson will need to identify if it is a unique opportunity with the follow up question.

----------------------------------------------------------------

"Expressive" Customer: *"No I've got my heart set on that black one."*

The caller has now indicated that, not only are they visual in nature but also kinaesthetic and in fulfilling their "hearts desire," price becomes less of an obstacle. Expressive people wear their heart on their sleeves; they are very open with people and expect the same in return.

----------------------------------------------------------------

Salesperson: *"OK. You're going to love it. It drives as well as it looks; what attracted you to this car and what are you driving at the moment?*

The salesperson continues to use visual language and incorporates kinaesthetic statements that have movement (driving). Expressive people are relatively easy to sell to and the salesperson has made an assumption that the customer will be driving the car shortly.

---

"Expressive" Customer: *"Well I've got a three year old Ford Focus which has been great but I really like the sporty look of the Astra, a friend has got one and I was really impressed."*

The customer is using the past tense so they have already made a decision that they will be changing. Image is the number one priority and they have reinforced the "ego" status by seeking to be the same as his friend.

---

Salesperson: *"I completely understand and don't worry about a deal at this stage; what we need to do is get you driving the car to make sure it feels right and take a good look at your car. So how quickly can you come down later on today or tomorrow?"*

The deal is not the critical point in this transaction. It is about desire and treating the customer in a friendly way. The "Expressive" personalities often make quick decisions but their attention span is low so getting them to act swiftly is important.

-------------------------------------------------------------

## ANALYTICAL

The character traits of an analytical personality are easily recognised. They wear clothes that are bland; they do not make strong eye contact and give you very little facial feedback. They walk slowly and precisely. Typically they will be in a role where accuracy and accountability matter (accountants; software engineers; librarians; teachers; civil servants) They'll have completed a substantial amount of homework or have good knowledge of their subject matter. They dislike social interaction so may appear very aloof or insular and they certainly won't want to talk about irrelevant matters. They are very task orientated and they will challenge your knowledge on any subject.

Because of their auditory nature; when you call them on the telephone they will listen intently and give you almost no acknowledgements or response, so it becomes difficult to know if they are actually listening at all. They will take longer to respond to each sentence as they are formulating their precise reply. They dislike a strong sales approach and will have no qualms in cutting across you and bluntly ending the call (after all they never want to be your friend!) You need to adopt a very different and logical approach for this type of person.

Dealing with the analytical type can prove to be the biggest challenge for natural salespeople, because they are almost exact opposites. A natural salesperson will want to make friends and talk about creative solutions to problems. The analytical person requires facts, logic and proof. The good news is, when you finally create the trust and bond with this type of personality, they become very loyal and only want to deal with you. (It's too painful to have to start the relationship with another salesperson)

When an analytical person calls about the same car, the approach will be different again:

Salesperson: *"Hello you are through to John Smith in sales, how can I help you?"*

-----------------------------------------------------------

"Analytical" Customer: *"Yes, I would like to know a little more about the black Vauxhall Astra registration number BG64 BXH; the 1.6 sport that's advertised on your website."*

There is unlikely to be any use of the salesperson's name. They will talk slowly in a precise manner and use details about the car in question. They have not expressed a specific request for information they are more likely waiting to test the knowledge and competency of the salesperson before moving forward with the enquiry.

Salesperson: ***"Yes I know the one I was involved with the sale when we brought the car into stock. It's a 1.6 turbo the more powerful of the two engines available. May I ask, is it just that particular vehicle or one in that price range that is of interest and if so what specifically do you want to know about the car?***

The "Analytical" person seeks proof, logic and guarantees. The salesperson is demonstrating product knowledge and an intimate understanding of the car in question. There is likely to be a very specific feature or reason that the analytical person is looking for in the product and they want reassurance of this before moving forward with the enquiry.

"Analytical" Customer: ***"Well you've already answered one question as it is the turbo version that I may have an interest in. So will this car have the new flexible seating in the rear. Can you explain the warranty that comes with this vehicle?***

"Analytical" people often have many questions and they already have significant product knowledge. They will give very little indication of buying at this stage as they want to satisfy all of the logical requirements first.

Salesperson: *"You are correct about the seating. As far as the warranty is concerned you get the balance of manufacturer warranty plus an additional year from our dealership. This is a full mechanical and electrical policy and will cover you for all items other than wear and tear. You also benefit from one year breakdown and recovery and the policy is for the car and not the driver so if someone else was driving and broke down, they would be covered."*

*"You've obviously done your homework and know specifically what you are looking for. We have had quite a few enquiries on this car since posting it on the website. Now the car may not be right for you, but I would recommend that you come down and have a look and bring with you your current car if you wish to part exchange. In that way you can inspect the car and make an informed decision on how to proceed. Would later on today or tomorrow be better for you?*

Analytical people do not respond well to "Picture Painting" nor do they appreciate feeling pushed into a decision. The salesperson continued to demonstrate good product knowledge and removed the threat of a sale by indicating the car may not be right for the customer. The language is very precise. But if the salesperson does not attempt to make the appointment, they will find themselves answering a catalogue of further questions. With "Analytical" people the salesperson will often find they are doing more of the talking.

## Summary - How to Deal With Behavioural Styles

| DEALING WITH DRIVERS | |
| --- | --- |
| Attributes | Actions |
| • Walk tall | ✓ Plan to ask questions and discuss specific actions and results |
| • Move with pace | |
| • Make strong eye contact | ✓ Use facts and logic |
| • Talk loud | ✓ When necessary, disagree with facts rather than opinions |
| • Task orientated | |
| • Forceful | |
| • Demanding | ✓ Keep it business-like, efficient and to the point |
| • Short attention span | |
| • Demand results | ✓ Personal guarantees and testimonials are least effective, better to provide opinions and facts |
| • Dislike weakness | |
| | ✓ Do not invade personal space |

## DEALING WITH EXPRESSIVES

| Attributes | Actions |
|---|---|
| • Walk with confidence | ✓ Seek opinions in areas you wish to develop to achieve mutual understanding |
| • Use gestures | |
| • Make good eye contact | |
| • Friendly | ✓ Discussion should be people as well as fact orientated |
| • Good facial feedback | |
| • Interested in others | |
| • Accommodating | ✓ Keep summarising |
| • Short attention span | ✓ Try short, fast moving experience stories |
| • Talkative | |
| • Dislike confrontation | ✓ Make sure to pin them down in a friendly way |
| • Use visual languages | |
| | ✓ Remember to discuss the future as well as the present |

## DEALING WITH AMIABLES

| Attributes | Actions |
| --- | --- |
| • Walk slouched | ✓ Work jointly, seek common ground |
| • Move slowly | ✓ Find out about personal interests and family |
| • Make reasonable eye contact | ✓ Be patient and avoid going for what looks like an easy pushover |
| • Friendly | |
| • Good facial feedback | ✓ Use personal assurances and avoid options and possibilities |
| • Interested in others | |
| • Very accommodating | ✓ Take time to be agreeable |
| • Don't want to upset people | ✓ Focus discussions on "HOW" |
| • Make slow decisions | |
| • Dislike confrontation | ✓ Demonstrate low risk solutions |
| • Won't take risks | |

## DEALING WITH ANALYTICALS

| Attributes | Actions |
|---|---|
| • Walk upright | ✓ Take action rather than words to demonstrate helpfulness and willingness |
| • Move slowly | |
| • Make poor eye contact | |
| • Aloof | ✓ Stick to specifics |
| • Little facial feedback | ✓ Their decisions are based upon facts and logic and they avoid risk |
| • No interest in small talk | |
| • Use tonal language and talk precisely | ✓ The can be co-operative, but established relationships take time |
| • No fear of upsetting people | |
| • Make slow decisions | ✓ Respond well to guarantees and official information |
| • Dislike confrontation | |
| • Won't take risks | ✓ Do not pressurise |

## Ask a Stupid Question

I'm sure this will have happened to you many times when you walk into a shop or any sales environment and you're asked by the salesperson *"May I help you?"* Your predictable response is probably *"No; just looking thank you!"* It's predictable because you were asked a closed question, which begs a yes or no response and it's the natural defensive position of any customer who is unsure of the salesperson.

There's 'nothing wrong' with closed questions at the meet and greet stage; but this salesperson used the wrong one. Imagine the situation is a car showroom; the question could be changed to *"Do you know very much about (car brand)?"* If this gets a yes response, it opens up a conversation; if no, it can be followed up with *"Is it just this particular model you're interested in?"* Assuming this gets a yes response the question style can be changed to "open" *"Tell me more about what you're after"* A further closed question can then be used; *"Have you been to our dealership before?"* if the response is no; the salesperson can shake hands and formally introduce themselves.

Language is very important in order to control the customer. Salespeople are generally in control if they can get the customer doing most of the talking; especially in the early stages. Remember, in order to sell something, you must first find a problem to solve; so the skill of the salesperson is to uncover the problems; to increase the urgency to do something about the problem and then to provide their solution. There are a number of different questioning styles to be employed; each of which creates a different outcome.

## OPEN

An open question; ***"How are you today?"*** will gain a fuller response and get the customer talking. Clearly in the early stages of conversation, these are important and they allow the salesperson to take control. Open questions are often prefixed with; WHO; WHAT; WHERE; WHY; HOW and WHEN.

## CLOSED

Closed questions will always gain a yes or no response and gain commitment. ***"Do you want to go ahead?"*** ***"Have you been into our restaurant before?"*** You should ask a closed question whenever you need to gain commitment or when you want to control the customer to the next point of conversation.

> "Clearly in the early stages of conversation, open questions are important and allow the salesperson to take control. Open questions are often prefixed with; WHO; WHAT; WHERE; WHY; HOW and WHEN."

## ALTERNATIVE

An alternative question style is where you offer up one of two alternatives. ***"Would you like the red one or the blue one?" "Morning or afternoon?" "Is it cash or card?"*** This style of question directs the customer to pick one of the two choices and allows the salesperson to control what happens next.

## LEADING

A leading question is where you already know the answer and you are guiding the customer to agree with you. ***"You said you liked the blue one didn't you?" "That's going to be really important for you, isn't it?"*** Seeking agreement throughout the sales conversation builds value and shows that you have been listening.

## VALUE LOADED

I describe a value loaded question as one where you add your opinion, or a third party opinion, to sway the customer to agree. ***"I like the blue one; don't you?" "Most of our customers are doing it this way because it is the most economical way, wouldn't you agree?"***

You need to exercise a certain amount of caution when employing a value loaded question, because it will work very well on "amiable" and "expressive" personality types; but it will not work at all with "driver" or those of an "analytical" nature.

## MULTIPLE

Multiple question styles are, as the title suggests, several questions all at once. **"Do you want the red one or the blue one?" "When do you want to take delivery?" "How will you be paying?"** These are very confusing for the customer and normally happen because the salesperson goes into panic mode and feels the need to fill any silent gaps in conversation with another question. They are used very effectively by trained journalists and politicians. Often, they will have several questions to pitch at their counterpart and they know they only have a limited timeframe or opportunity to ask them.

## REFLECTIVE

Reflective questions are all about summarising (reflecting back) on the conversation to demonstrate that you have been actively listening and to bring the sale to a point of conclusion. **"So you're happy with blue?" "The minimum number you require is 10,000?" "You must have them in 4 weeks?" "And we're unable to deliver at the West Gate entrance; that's right?" "I think we can manage that... let's do it"**

## Find the Pain...Then Sell the Gain

Passengers on the "London Underground" will be familiar with the announcement *"Mind the Gap."* They are of course referring to the gap between the platform and the train. As this is generally a small gap, it is insignificant and most passengers pay little attention, hence the announcement.

On the other hand if the gap was four foot wide and a hundred foot deep, they would take notice. This analogy can be applied in sales to demonstrate the gap between the customer's current situation and the future position.

Imagine you are selling screws to contractors in the building industry. You have an appointment to talk to the buyer of a large construction company who currently uses a slightly inferior but cheaper imported screw from abroad.

During qualification you have identified that the failure rate on the screws from the current supplier can vary significantly from batch to batch and on occasion they have been let down on the deliveries.

Your role as a salesperson is to drive a wedge into this "small gap" in order to widen it, increasing the pain and making it more significant before you present your product as the solution to this increased problem. This is how the conversation may play out:

**Pain:**
Salesperson: *"So when you have batches of screws that don't meet the required standards, presumably you have to take down your partition walls and start again, is that right?"*

Customer: *"Yes because we have strict fire regulations to adhere to"*

Salesperson: *"So that will have a direct impact on profitability, because you will have to pay the workers twice and if that means you are running late on the contract you may incur penalty charges?*

Customer: *"It has happened once or twice."*

Salesperson: *"Can you recall the last time the deliveries were late?*

Customer: *"Earlier this year we had a bit of a problem."*

Salesperson: *"What happened?"*

Customer: *"There was a hold up at the docks for a day and a half"*

Salesperson *"I have no idea what you are paying your workers but if they were unable to get on with the job, I would imagine that would be very frustrating and expensive"*

**Gain:**

Salesperson *"Whilst our screws are slightly more expensive, they are made from a higher grade of steel and within extremely high tolerances. This means we have a failure rate under fire test conditions of 0.001% which is market leading. Of course this means that our customers rarely experience problems on site and the workers are pleased because they get less damage and wastage. That would be important to your company too I suppose?"*

Customer: *"Anything to keep the workforce from moaning would be a bonus."*

Salesperson: *"You are also aware that we produce our products in purpose built factories here in this Country with distribution outlets North and South. This means we can guarantee next day deliveries right across the range and if necessary in emergencies we have courier drivers who will deliver. So there are no excuses for holding up the job. That would be useful too wouldn't you agree?"*

Customer: *"Of course."*

Salesperson *"Let me show you our proposal to supply your company in a way that will reduce costs and improve customer satisfaction."*

When we finally make a decision to buy something we've normally reached a tipping point where the need for change outweighs the cost or consequences of making the decision. (The pain has been increased enough to make the gain worthwhile)

I remember moving house many years ago with my young family and we plumbed our old washing machine into the new kitchen. I was a bit disappointed because the machine looked tired and shabby and it detracted from the sparkling new units. There was nothing mechanically wrong with the machine so my motivation for change was small. One day, not long after the move, the door of the machine snapped away from its hinges as we loaded it full with dirty clothes. Suddenly my motivation for change had increased; I was in no mind to make a repair and with three children changing clothes frequently each day, I went shopping.

I recall it was a weekend and our local retail park where the electrical retailers fought their battles, was very busy. Parking the car was a challenge but that was only the start.

There was a fine selection of machines available and I did my best to make sense of the information at hand. The capacity of the machine was clearly going to be important, given our growing family requirements. Then there was the spin cycle and the power output and the number of stars awarded by "Which" magazine and of course, the price.

I explained to the salesperson that we have three children and needed a reliable and efficient machine. Today. I pointed to a particular one and asked his opinion and whether he could recommend something better. He appeared quite knowledgeable and with growing confidence I allowed him to guide me to a superior machine at a similar price. OK. *"We'll take it," I announced"; if you can help me to the car".*

*"I'm sorry sir, we don't carry stock of this machine, but I can order it and you'll have it in the next two weeks"* The

salesperson hadn't listened carefully to my requirements and two weeks was out of the question.

I needed something right now. So with further qualification of what was available from stock and a debate over the merits of each machine, I finally bought a much more expensive unit. The price wasn't the most important aspect. The gap between my current circumstance (no machine and piles of washing) and paying more than I expected, had been bridged.

My tipping point had been reached.

## System! Process! Plan! Who Needs Them?

**"If you put them in the wrong way up; they'll never grow"**
I was probably about eight years old and I adored my
Grandpa. He was a giant of a man. I suppose most people
are when you're eight! He once had a fine head of hair
according the black and white family photographs scattered
around the house, but now there were a few long strands
of greying locks slapped tightly to his head with a dab of
Brylcreem. His face was rugged and the skin on his hands
was cracked; fingernails were full of soil. This was a man,
born in a generation of hard work and graft. He was a
bricklayer by trade and in spite of enduring two world wars
had built a small but successful company building houses
in the local area. He was hugely respected by friends and
colleagues for being a generous man; (a point my Grandma
always reminded him of when outstanding money was not
forthcoming.) We had a special relationship; I could spend
hours listening to his stories and marvel at his practical skills
building a greenhouse or repairing a gate.

We were together planting potatoes and my job was to
carefully place the seed potatoes into the finely sifted
trenches of soil. Grandpa said "If you put them the wrong
way up, they'll never grow" It was a slow meticulous
process of clearing stones from the soil troughs as they
would impede the growth of the shoots and roots. Each
seed potato was surrounded by soft earth and generously
watered. In weeks to come, when they spouted through
the surface, it would take care and attention to build a
supporting wall of soil so the flowering shrubs stood tall. All

good tradesmen will tell you it's the preparation that counts and taking time at this point will pay dividends later.

If you think about it, there's a process for everything. Baking the perfect chocolate cake requires you to use the best ingredients, in the right proportions, mixed in a certain way and baked for just the right amount of time. Alter any of these elements and the cake just doesn't turn out right.

High Street retailers are all too familiar with the importance of processes and structure. McDonalds is possibly the most iconic franchise in the world and its success has been built from the reputation of exemplary standards and attention to detail. Customers feel comfortable and relaxed when visiting a McDonalds anywhere in the world because it provides them with a level of consistency.

Consistency is a key ingredient for consumers when making a decision because it removes the element of risk. Most of us would probably visit McDonalds even if we could buy a cheaper burger from a van outside the football ground. I spend a lot of time travelling in the UK and Premier Inn provides me with a known quantity and a level of commitment that makes me feel relaxed.

So why is it; when we talk about a sales process, that salespeople believe they have this wonderful sixth sense and tell you that every customer is different and they make it up as they go along? Of course all customers are different but successful salespeople have a very rigid approach using their communication skills to manipulate the customer to follow their path.

If there is a sales process to follow when you are face to face with a customer, then there's an even more important process to follow when you are using the telephone; because the visual elements are missing.

In chapter four I'm going to explain the exact process that has worked for many of my clients helping them make thousands of appointments. It is a SYSTEM to follow so you can add your own charisma and style in order to create your own bespoke calls.

## Research Your Target

*"If you haven't done your homework, then I think we're done here!"*

I wanted the ground to open up and swallow me. I was facing a formidable man; a senior director of a major UK leasing company and someone with a reputation for ruthless business efficiency. It hadn't been easy to get this meeting; it had taken several weeks to finally navigate the appointment through his personal assistant and the time slot had been allocated with military precision. Now here I was about to blow it in the opening minutes and possibly to learn one of the most important lessons of my sales career.

He was sitting in the dominant chair, slightly elevated from my position and across the width of an enormous desk. You would describe him as an elegant man, immaculately dressed in a light blue suit, with contrasting shirt and tie; the cufflinks were clearly expensive and his aftershave heavy with wood spice. He clutched my business card, unceremoniously tapping it on the desk; his fingernails were manicured and as he delivered that sentence he slipped into a confident but forced smile; he knew he was in control and he was exercising his right to prove it.

My mistake was not to take enough notice of the characteristics of my prospect. He was a "Driver" personality; dominant in every way and a foolish slip into my normal style of rapport building was to ask **"Tell me more about the organisation and your role"**

Of course I had done my homework. I knew everything I could possibly know about the group; their financial position, the number of staff, the latest results and all of the recent press. I had created my meeting based upon a perceived need for training and I had set the meeting up accordingly. Fortunately for me, I was able to recover the situation and turn the conversation round. I even sold them a sizable training contract.

It was a valuable lesson in preparation. Remember you can only sell solutions to problems and in some cases the organisation or individual you are dealing with do not know they even have a problem before your approach. Whenever I approach a prospective client I make sure I know as much as I can about them. Information is free and easy; more readily available now than ever before.

Utilise the company website, search Linked-In and all social media; read press reports and company updates. Examine the profile of your decision maker (it's amazing what you can find out through google!)

If your audience is small / medium sized businesses and the decision maker is the owner / driver, then information may not be so forthcoming; but you can research their field of expertise.

Imagine for a moment your job is to sell vans and light commercial vehicles. How many "White Vans" have we encountered on the motorways? You can rightly assume the market for this type of vehicle is massive.

So who needs a van?

The list is endless. Delivery drivers; florists; builders; plumbers; electricians; butchers bakers and candlestick makers.

If you are of a certain age, you will recall that in times gone by, in the UK, "Yellow Pages" was THE directory of choice. It had every business listing in an area; classified and re-classified into sections with alphabetical listings and opportunities for companies to stand out with a bigger advert than their competitor. Full page Yellow Pages advertisements were very expensive and formed a big part of many company's marketing budget.

This was also a great source of business opportunity. I recall working with a company selling vans and their sales team were struggling to find fresh sales leads. Randomly, they were looking for any company in their area who used vans to make their approach. Naturally the success rate was quite low and demotivating. I suggested that we start by looking at "Yellow Pages" in the classification section and highlighting what sort of organisation may have the need for their products. Clearly architects, accountants and zoo keepers did not fall into the category. However there was more possibility with florists, delivery companies, builders and electricians.

This sub-classification was useful, but still not productive enough. Most builders are one man bands; so too are those people delivering flowers; so to sell to this group of people would be slow and unproductive. What they needed to do was to look for bigger organisations that used vans as part of their daily routine. Double glazing and conservatory companies must have the need to transport glass and components. Looking under this classification opens up a myriad of companies all in a competitive market with a need to have reliable vans on the road 24/7. They have to move stuff around and are probably owned by one or two decision makers. If you can sell to these companies; they will probably quite happily refer you on to business acquaintances (who are in the same industry) after all, where they buy their vans from won't impact on company performance. The results were dramatically different in a positive way.

You have to "Pick Your Fights." You need to understand your marketplace and why what you are doing is different from the rest; whether that's on value or innovation. Only in this way can you effectively target your audience for the approach.

## The Salesperson's Mind-Set

A client recently remarked *"I understand the importance of preparation, but how do I overcome my fear of actually getting started"*

I fully understand these fears and here are a few positive tips to adopt:

- Make telephone prospecting a daily routine

- Imagine the positive outcome and the results you will get from calling (glass half full not empty)

- You already know far more about your subject matter than the listener, so don't be nervous

- If you were to receive good news from a phone call, would you react positively? I would.

- Don't make sales calls in front of your colleagues or customers. Find a quiet spot and make your calling session last for 40-45 minutes. (we all have a natural attention span for doing a task and it does take a period of time to get into the prospecting zone)

- Stand up. It improves voice projection.

- Smile as you dial! The upbeat voice quality will be understood at the other end

- Deliver the message as if you were talking to an intelligent 12 year old. This was a tip given to me by a reporter from Sky News. Very appropriate, I thought.

- What's the worst that can happen? Possibly the word "NO".

"Don't make sales calls in front of your colleagues or customers. Find a quiet spot and make your calling session last for 40-45 minutes."

# PREPARATION-SUMMARY

- Understanding your WHY. The passion and belief that will make you stand out

- People do more to avoid pain than they do to create pleasure. This is a powerful motivator when decisions are made

- Does your offer or proposition pass the B.E.V.A. test?

- Are you ready to adapt to present to the four personality types of prospect?

- Have you crafted your offer using the right style of questions so you maintain control of the conversation?

- Have you researched your prospect?

# Chapter Two: Proposition

**What is it you want people to know about? What is it you do? What's the message they need to hear? Your proposition should be a clear and concise statement, so in a nutshell, the decision maker can agree to see you or buy your product or service.**

But remember, people don't buy WHAT you do; they buy WHY you do it. So your message must trigger a gut decision. When we present something in a way where the other person can only make a rational decision, you are presenting it to the thinking part of the brain and, the highest level of confidence they can give this is I *think* this is the right decision. When we make gut decisions we are doing something that *feels* right even in the face of conflicting logical evidence. When you ask most successful business people and entrepreneurs; what makes them successful, they will often tell you they *"trust their gut"* and the times that they have listened to advice and logical reasoning from others is where they have fallen down.

If you cannot describe Why you do What you do; then it will be impossible for anyone else to understand it.

Take yourself back to a party you may have attended; the drinks are flowing and you are doing the social circuit chatting to different people in the room. You decide to freshen your drink and upon your return, the group of people you were talking to are engrossed in conversation and you find yourself slightly outside the circle. Glancing around, you make brief eye contact with another social outcast and even though you don't want to start a conversation, they make a move towards you.

*"Great party don't you think? I'm Brian"* You just know, when Brian goes for the formal handshake, that this could be hard work and refreshing your drink now seemed like a really bad idea. The next minute or so are spent discussing who you know at the party; who's related to whom and meaningless conversations about people you are never likely to meet again. Then there's that moment of silence.

Most of us are not good with silences and a natural question to break the ice might be; *"So what is it you do Brian?"*

*"I'm an independent financial advisor. I've been doing it for over twenty years and boy, have I seen some changes in that time. I mainly do pensions work and life cover, but if you're ever in the need for a new mortgage; then I'm your man! I get a lot of my business through friends of friends"*

Brian had adopted his sales pose: confident, feet apart, one hand in his pocket and talking too loud.

Now you're losing the will to live. Brian's in full flow telling you **what** he does. Now let's change Brian's response to the question.

*"For the last twenty years I've been fortunate enough to do something I really love and enjoy. I help people make more money for themselves and their families and to make sure they can have the lifestyle they deserve. Because they are so comfortable with my approach; they tend to recommend a lot of friends and family onto me, which is great"*

This time Brian is explaining **Why** he's doing what he does. I don't know about you, but I know which Brian I would prefer to talk to!

You may have heard this described as your "Elevator Pitch". When this concept was first described to me, it was a light bulb moment and a wake-up call in the way I'd been presenting myself previously. Imagine one day a person steps into the elevator with you and presses the button for floor 10. This person is one you have been frantically trying to gain an appointment with. Desperate to say hello and introduce yourself, you now only have the time it takes to reach floor ten to say the right words to impress them enough so you can agree to a further meeting. This gives complete clarity to the actions you must take.

The structure I adopt when thinking about my "Elevator Pitch" is based around the problems people face and the pain that can cause them versus a solution. (The before and after scenario) Of course I also passionately believe that what I do will get them the results they deserve.

I utilise a basic 4 step process:

| PROBLEM | SOLUTION |
|---|---|
| 1. You know how.... | 3. What we do.... |
| 2. Which means that.... | 4. Which means that.... |

Let me give you an example using my training business.

**You know how...**
*"People don't choose to fail, so when they do they become frustrated, demotivated and stressed"*

**Which means that...**
*"They lack direction and confidence; they can cost their organisations money and lose out on the rewards they deserve"*

**What we do...**
*"Is to coach them so they can discover their hidden talents and abilities and steer them towards their true potential"*

**Which means that...**
*"Their organisations benefit from the talent they employed and together they can achieve sustained success"*

Obviously, when I'm describing this to someone, it becomes more conversational and focusses on WHY I'm in business.

*"I'm a huge believer that people don't choose to fail and when I see them struggling to achieve its sad because they become frustrated, demotivated and stressed. They lose confidence and direction; it can cost their organisations money and they lose out on the rewards they deserve."*

*"I coach them on a one to one level to help them discover their, often hidden, talents and abilities and steer them towards their true potential. It's a fantastic feeling for me and for them as they develop and become more productive. The organisation benefits from the real talent they employed and together they achieve sustainable success"*

I applied the same technique to give clarity as to why I created my telephone prospecting programme and the reason for this book, explaining my system.

*"So many people seem to struggle with the telephone and I was one of them. It frustrated me with the lack of help and support I could find to help me make sales calls and the rejection I felt when I made them badly."*

*"Which meant that not only was I losing out on potential sales, costing me a fortune; but I also hated the part of the job that was absolutely essential if I was going to be successful?"*

*"Finally, with perseverance, a lot of pain and thousands of calls later; I found a way to make successful sales calls on a consistent basis and I created a SYSTEM; a template for others to follow"*

*"This means that anyone following my SYSTEM can not only guarantee much higher call conversions, saving time and effort; but also to spend more time FACE TO FACE with decision makers making more money"*

What I'm describing here is the "Elevator Pitch" as I would explain it face to face with a potential client. Later in the book we will look at how you alter your basic proposition to make it fit a telephone approach.

To sanity check your proposition we can see if it passes the **B.E.V.A.** Test. First of all, in the last example were there sufficient BENEFITS for the client?

- Sales support
- SYSTEM to follow
- Saving time and effort

- Greater successes
- Less painful
- More client meetings
- Potentially greater sales and more money

Did the proposition have an element of EMOTION?

- Struggle & frustrations
- Hate, fear & rejection
- Pain
- Breakthrough
- Success
- Relief

Can the potential client work out if what you are saying has a VALUE to them?

This is only your opening introduction and whilst you don't want to go into too much detail, the proposition should indicate a value offer. We will look at the "Contrast Principle" shortly to build on the value; but for now it contains:

- Cost of burning sales leads
- Cost of time badly spent
- More efficient call conversion
- More sales and more money

The final part of **B.E.V.A.** is to ASK for the business or deliver the call to action, which may be a further meeting.

The current propositions above don't go that far but it is a natural and easy step:

> *"This means that anyone following my SYSTEM can not only guarantee much higher call conversions, saving time and effort; but also to spend more time FACE TO FACE with decision makers making more money"*

> *"I'm sure there are people in your business who would really benefit from this and generate the company a huge amount of incremental profit. If you have half an hour free in your diary I can explain things in more detail so you're in a position to make an informed choice; are you free on Tuesday or Wednesday this week?"*

## Contrast Principle

I mentioned earlier the thought process behind the contrast principle and the need to make the biggest gap possible between the client's current situation and the future position. Following on from my last proposition example; this could be one of the ways I create the contrast principle and this may happen at a subsequent meeting or immediately after going through the proposition if the clients asks for more detail.

*"When I first started in sales, one of the skills I really lacked was my ability to pick up the telephone and to prospect new business. This wasn't down to a lack of effort, more to a lack of training and knowing what to say. I really struggled and many salespeople that I meet say the same thing"*

*"I wonder how many sales each of your sales team are losing out on, each month, because of their inability to pick up the telephone and to prospect? Would it be 5 sales per month? 2 sales? 3 sales?*

**RESPONSE:**
*"It's probably at least "3".*
*"And you said you currently have 25 salespeople so that's 75 sales per month you are missing."*
*"Typically, how much profit do you make on each sale would it be £500? £1,500? £1,000?*

**RESPONSE:**
*"We average just over £1,000.*
You continue:
*"So £75,000 of PROFIT each month is £900,000 a year and unless you change the way they are approaching this; it could cost you almost two million in lost profits in the next couple of years"*
*"May I just run through exactly what we can do, in a really cost effective way, to completely turn this around and add that value onto your bottom line?"*

The principle doesn't always have to have a financial contrast; it may be an emotional cost. For example if the industry you are working in is about people's lives and caring.

By way of other working examples, I've taken three sales scenarios so you can see how the process can be followed adapting your approach on the requirements of the situation.

## Scenario 1:
• You manufacture and supply double glazing units

## Your Target Customers:
• Architects; building design companies; local government housing projects

## Unique Selling Points:
• Highest standards of energy efficient glass in Europe. Glass can be supplied in the largest sheets available anywhere in UK. Can turnaround bespoke glazing in very short period of time

## Scenario 2
• You provide digital marketing solutions to companies

## Your Target Customers
• Small and medium sized companies in any field of work

**Unique Selling Points:**

- Great designers. Impressive results. Innovative ideas for lead generation. All "in house" one stop solution

---

**Scenario 3:**

You are a recruitment agency specialising in sales staff

**Your Target Customers:**

Medium to large scale companies with a sales force both internally and field based

**Unique Selling Points:**

Access to a substantial database of candidates with the latest search facilities. Tailored assessment centre programmes

---

The first stage in the creation of your proposition is to identify areas of issue for your potential client; to increase the pain this may be causing them and then to marry it up with the solution you can provide.

## Double Glazing Scenario

| Potential Issues or Problems | Cost or Impact on the Business | Your Solution |
|---|---|---|
| Using units that will fall behind industry standards for efficiency | Only the most up to date designers will be offered the prime contracts, meaning the company could lose out on revenue and profit | Your products are already at the highest standards |
| Buildings not as environmentally friendly or efficient as they should be | Selling buildings with the most efficient ways of saving energy is a unique selling point; without this; sales and reputation could be affected | Your products are the most efficient and you have savings comparisons over the building lifetime |
| Designs are currently limited by the available unit sizes in the UK | To stand out and differentiate from the competition. Uniqueness and innovation can normally command higher sales prices and recognition | Your panels have been part of design awards throughout Europe |
| Lead time for bespoke units can cause problems on project completion | Any delay in project completion normally attracts high penalty costs, directly effecting profitability | You are geared up for this type of work and have excellent customer satisfaction testimonials to back this up. |

Utilising the four stage process outlined above your proposition may be something like:

*"I'm sure you're aware of the restrictions in glass size currently available in the UK and the fact that if you want something a little bit different to make you stand out; then the lead time has traditionally been very long."*

*"Of course this means you are competing in the same marketplace with everyone else so you have to work harder to differentiate your company and probably operate on tighter margins to win your fair share of contracts"*

*"We have a state of the art factory here in the UK where we produce the most efficient glass panels in Europe to the latest specifications. Our glass can be produced in much larger sections and we can do that with an extremely quick turnaround from order"*

*"Architects have used our products to create award winning buildings, which has set them apart and allowed them to charge premium prices and to gain preferential status when tendering for new contracts"*

*"If you have an hour free in your diary I would like to introduce you to what we can offer so you have a choice with your designs moving forward; when is a good time for you Wednesday or Thursday next week?"*

## Digital Marketing Scenario

| Potential Issues or Problems | Cost or Impact on the Business | Your Solution |
|---|---|---|
| Companies have a web presence without clear direction for what they want to achieve | The web site should be a sales funnel and if it's not then the company is wasting money and losing out on potential sales | You work with clients on a tailored programme to get the best results out of digital marketing |
| Poor design and implementation means few people can find them | The cost of maintaining a web presence without suitable ranking means that they are losing out on sales and providing a negative image to potential customers | Your designers have won awards and have a clear plan on search engine optimisation |
| No mechanism for building a list of followers or on-going interaction with the company | The list is king! Most customers do not buy at the first point of contact but they may do so several months down the line if they remember you. Lost opportunity | You link together a clear programme using social media. You design the site to capture customer details so they can be nurtured |
| Unaware of what business they are missing through a lack of tracking | Failure to test what works and what doesn't means you can't correct mistakes or identify opportunities when they present themselves | You can monitor every stage of the process and react quickly to make subtle changes and track all leads through to a conclusion |

Your proposition may be something like:

*"We're all aware that the buying habits of customers have changed dramatically in recent years and the Internet is used not only to conduct research of products and services but to interact and to buy online"*

*"This means if companies don't have a joined up approach to digital marketing where they can drive traffic to the site, capture customer details and begin the relationship; they can lose out on thousands of pounds of lost revenue and worse still, project completely the wrong company image"*

*"Our award winning designers are experts in creating the complete package for clients specifically tailored to their business"*

*"Which means you can see measurable improvements in the volume of sales leads that come into your company; reduce the amount you spend on other marketing initiatives and guarantee that when customers look for companies like yours; you stand out"*

*"It will only take an hour of your time for me to show you what we do and how we've transformed other companies and helped them grow. Would Thursday or Friday be better for you?"*

## Recruitment Agency Scenario

| Potential Issues or Problems | Cost or Impact on the Business | Your Solution |
|---|---|---|
| Companies pay a lot to agencies especially when they have regular positions to fill | Big cost to the business and directly off the bottom line | Your assessment centre process is very cost effective |
| The choice of candidates is often limited and of poor quality | Taking on people that are substandard not only costs the agency fee but potential future business | You have the latest search facilities which means you can unearth candidates that other cannot |
| In spite of well written CV's some candidates struggle to perform in the role | By not testing their ability to do the job, companies pay for the initial recruitment and on-going induction training only for them to fail down the line | The assessment process test the candidates core competencies against a job brief from the company |
| All the agencies seem the same and charge similar prices | Little choice and held to ransom. The time and effort has a cost implication to the company | The process you adopt with the assessment centre approach takes one day of the clients time with lots of choice and low cost |

Your proposition may look like this:

*"Finding the right people for your business can be challenging and time consuming. Many companies who use agencies are fed up with the choice of candidates available"*

*"The costs can be high too, not only in the fee itself, but also in the interview time and the initial training time for candidates that sometimes don't work out"*

*"We do something completely different, by presenting you with a number of candidates all on one day and, assessing their ability to perform in the role all under the same test conditions."*
*"You are able to make an informed choice beyond their CV and decide on the right characters for your business. What's more, you can take on as many candidates as you like for one flat fee making it incredibly cost effective"*

*"If you have an hour available I can show you exactly how this works so you can make an informed decision on your recruitment policy moving forward. Is Wednesday or Thursday better for you?"*

Your proposition lies at the heart of your telephone approach so having a clear understanding of **WHY** you are in business will drive the **HOW** and the **What**.

# PROPOSITION-SUMMARY

- Remember, people don't buy WHAT you do; they buy WHY you do it, most decisions are made in the gut and not the head

- You sell solutions to problems; if the prospect is unaware of the problem, then you have to highlight it for them

- Utilise the "Contrast Principle"

- Follow the 4-stage process when creating your "Elevator Pitch"

# Chapter Three: P.I.C.T.U.R.E.

n an earlier chapter we discovered the communication model when face to face with others. When using the telephone, this model naturally alters:

| | | |
|---|---|---|
| Words | 7% | 18% |
| Voice Quality | 38% | 82% |
| ~~Body Language~~ | 55% | |

In the majority of cases; when we are not using video technology such as Skype or Face Time; the communication model lacks visual input and the model changes dramatically so that voice quality accounts for 82% of the delivery. How long do you think you have to make a favourable impression on the telephone? The answer is about 7 seconds.

During that time the customer is not really listening to your words, but simply tuning into your voice quality and deciding whether they like you or not. It sounds very simplistic, but just recall back to a call you may have received recently and as you picked up the phone, the following thoughts probably crossed your mind:

*"Who is this?"*
*"What do they want?*
*"Are they friendly?"*
*"Is it important?"*
*"Do I feel threatened?"*

It had been a great week! Three more deals closed off, some very happy clients and an unexpected opportunity to take the business in a different direction. It was a bright sunny morning and because I was early for my meeting; I'd decided to pull off the motorway and grab a well-earned cup of Earl Grey. (Not quite in the best china cup; more of a cardboard mug with a hole in the lid)

The radio news report was rudely interrupted by the car phone. It was not a number I recognised, so hopefully another bit of good client news.

*"Kevin Charlton"* I announced confidently.

**"Oh hello, is that Mr Charlton?"** The caller was slightly hesitant, perhaps a bit surprised by my immediate pick up.

*"Yes, that's right"* I replied with curiosity in my voice. There was a slight pause before he said

**"Can I ask if you're driving at the moment?"** This voice was serious and not the sort of bounce I would expect if it was a new client looking for help.

*"No, not at the moment"* I immediately started to feel apprehensive; had I done something wrong?

*"Mr Charlton"* The caller had more gravity in the voice now and he remained formal; most people would surely call me Kevin?

*"I'm Constable Taylor from North Tyneside police station"* My heart sank.

Regrettably, it was not good news. My father had been found in the hallway of his semi-detached house by the police earlier that morning having suffered a fatal heart attack. Not altogether unexpected but a shock none the less.

The point I make, is long before I knew the content of the call, my mind had performed a cartwheel of guessing games about the caller not based on the words exchanged, but on the sound of the voice.

The opening of the call sets the mood and knowing that the listener is battling against the self-talk in their head; your message has to pierce through the chatter; grab their attention and quickly present them with a benefit to focus upon. Not easy in the first few seconds.

In order to train and demonstrate the importance of voice quality of any outbound call; I utilise the acronym **PICTURE** to identify the important elements of voice:

# P    PITCH

The pitch of the voice is defined as the "rate of vibration of the vocal folds". The sound of the voice changes as the rate of vibrations varies. As the number of vibrations per second increases, so does the pitch, meaning the voice would sound higher. Faster rates form higher voices, or higher pitches, while slower rates elicit deeper voices, or lower pitches.

The vibrations, and the speed at which they vibrate, are dependent on the length and thickness of the vocal cords, as well as the tightening and relaxation of the muscles surrounding them. This explains why women generally have higher voices than men; women tend to have higher voices because they have shorter vocal cords. The length and thickness of the vocal cords, however, are not the only factors that affect one's pitch. The pitch of someone's voice can also be affected by emotions, moods and inflection. Interestingly, our emotions can also affect the pitch of our voices. When people become frightened or excited, the muscles around the voice box (or larynx) unconsciously contract, putting strain on the vocal cords, making the pitch higher.

So it is the pitch of the voice; the physical changes in vocal cord length, which is the science behind the sound. It is the interpretation of the sound, however that gives meaning to the words and phrases and this is directly influenced by a change in voice inflection. We tend not to take high squeaky voices very seriously so when you are prospecting (and possibly feeling nervous) take deep breaths before you call. This will have the effect of calming the body and stopping the pitch from rising too high.

# I    INFLECTION

We can change the inflection of the voice by altering the pitch of the sound (shortening the vocal cords to make the sound higher or lengthening them to make the sound lower)

I describe this as the interest factor in the voice. When an Australian is talking to you the inflection towards the end of a phrase or sentence often goes up, making it sound as though they are asking you a question. When people feel they are being asked a question, they listen more to the words. However, if the questioning inflection is at the end of almost every sentence; it can become quite irritating and it loses meaning.

Natural accents carry an inflection that can maintain the interest of the listener. If you think about how the people from Wales sound; or the Scots, Irish, Scouse or Geordies; they are often perceived to have a more caring and warm inflection in the voice.  Research also indicates that Geordie or Scots accents are perceived to be class-less compared to people from the South of England and therefore it is no co-incidence that many call centres have been re-located to these areas from abroad. Callers in centres outside of the UK may cost less and the staff have impeccable manners and grasp of the English language, but a lack of the correct inflection in a sentence can change the meaning dramatically and can confuse people.

Consider the sentence below and read it out aloud with the emphasis on the word in bold text and see how it can change the context of the sentence:

*"**I** didn't say you were speeding"*
*"I **didn't** say you were speeding"*
*"I didn't **say** you were speeding"*
*"I didn't say **you** were speeding"*
*"I didn't say you **were** speeding"*
*"I didn't say you were **speeding**"*

See what I mean?

The inflection in the voice will be translated in many ways by the listener. They will hear inquisitiveness, urgency, concern, empathy, excitement and so forth. When you are calling it is important to tell an engaging story.

If you think about how the people from Wales sound; or the Scots, Irish, Scouse or Geordies; they are often perceived to have a more caring and warm inflection in the voice."

Do you recall when you were a young child and your Mum or Dad would read a bedtime story?

Just one more branch and Jack would be at the top.

"Mustn't look down" he thought. He was scared. Jack had climbed some big trees before but nothing like this beanstalk. His hands were sore from gripping onto thick leaves and his legs were heavy.

Peering through the screen of green Jack could see a bright light. Was it sunshine? Had he climbed so high he had gone through the clouds?

Heaving himself with the last ounce of strength from the top branch he crawled through the opening of a new land. He flopped onto solid earth, face down in the sandy soil. It smelt just like meadow where he milked the cows, fresh and clean.

Beads of sweat were running into his eyes as he sat up to look around. Rubbing them away he started to focus, it didn't feel like sunshine anymore. As Jack looked up he stared at big thick scaly trunks of what he thought were trees, but to his horror as he slowly lifted his head he froze.

The bright light wasn't coming from the sun; it was a huge ball of fire, bellowing from the mouth of an enormous DRAGON! Jack couldn't move. He wanted to scream....

When I read similar stories to my children I would make it sound real. They were in the moment. They could feel Jack's strength sapping away and the relief as he finally made it to the top. The sincerity in the story has to come through to make the child believe. Similarly, the sincerity of your call to a prospective customer has to carry the same gravitas and the inflection in your voice plays a very big part in this process.

## C    COURTESY

There's nothing worse than a rude caller, so it goes without saying that you should always be courteous when making an outbound call.

Sometimes a lack of call structure can be perceived as a lack of courtesy. I'm sure you have found yourself on the receiving end of an unsolicited call from a call centre and the overriding feeling when taking these calls is they are intrusive, demanding and generally rude.

I'm sure when the companies set out to make the calls, they are well intentioned and it may be they are offering a fantastic service or product that will appeal to many.

Unfortunately, partly because of the bad press these types of calls have received and partly because a lack of targeting (there is no need for a conservatory for someone living in a 7th floor apartment block); they are often cut short by the listener. But there is another reason for cutting these calls short and that is because they have not gained permission to continue with the call and they are simply calling at an inconvenient time.

It will no doubt be argued by the large call centres, that by seeking this "GREEN LIGHT" they are going to receive a lot of negative responses and this may indeed be the case. However, the alternative is they are less professional. They continue with the call regardless; have the call terminated and create a poor impression of the organisation in the eyes of a potential customer.

As you will have gathered from chapter one on preparation, I believe if you are to have the highest degree of calling success, then you need to target your audience. Part of this preparation will often involve what I call a "SUSPECT" call. The difference between a "SUSPECT" and a "PROSPECT" is to identify those people who have absolutely no need for your offer or service compared to those that may be interested at a point sometime in the future.

As I was writing this chapter today, I received such a call (albeit rather crudely applied)

*"Hello, can I speak to the person in your company that deals with your waste management please"*

If my company (Steer Coaching & Development) was an engineering or building organisation, it may be that we have a problem to solve with regard to waste management. As a training provider, working on a consultancy basis, I don't have such a need.

Rather than presupposing that I would have a need, the question could have been asked:

*"Hello, my name is XXXXXX from XXXXXX, just a quick question may I ask if your company has the need for industrial waste management services?"*

Now on the basis that a quick look at my website would have prevented the call completely; at least this would have been an effective "SUSPECT" call. If I did have a need for such a service; I then fall into the category of "PROSPECT". The **SYSTEM** I have put together is for you to make the most from "PROSPECT" calls.

Going back to the "GREEN LIGHT" and seeking permission to continue, all I mean is to introduce a sentence early in the call to ensure that you are OK to continue. This is often as simple as **"Are you OK to talk for a moment?"** or some people prefer to use the negative connotation "**I haven't caught you at a bad time have I?"** on the basis that psychologically the customer is ready to say the word NO! My personal preference is to use the first one, because we don't need to try and catch the listener out.

The main purpose of the "GREEN LIGHT" is to gain control of the call. You normally receive one of three responses:

1. *"No I'm busy"*
*"Not a problem, when is the best time to call you back"* This will gain you a date and time and give you the permission you require.

2. *"What's it about?"*
You have now gained permission to continue and control the call.

3. *"Yes carry on"*
You now have permission.

Courtesy is very important, but it does not mean your call has to be weak, pleading or desperate; far from it. But if you are going to start a relationship with a client, then it needs to position you as the professional. The quality of your initial approach may well set the scene for future negotiations so adopt the "Moral High Ground"

## T   TONE

I often describe the tone of the voice as the meaning attached to the words or the type of sound that someone makes with their voice in a particular situation. We understand when someone is talking in a monotone voice and the impression can be "Boring". In the sporting world, the famous tennis player, Andy Murray has even ridiculed himself for having a boring monotone voice.

The meaning of the words can change depending on the sentence, however, by way of example, try saying aloud the following words, with their exact meaning (Believable in a believable tone of voice etc.)

**BELIEVABLE**
**HONEST**
**HAPPY**
**SAD**
**ANGRY**
**SEXY**

When saying the word "Believable" with true meaning we tend to break each syllable down as if to empathise the importance of the whole word.

Honest can have the inflection rise or fall depending on the meaning in the sentence in the head of the speaker. It is very difficult to be truly happy and say the word without smiling. It takes a lot of facial muscles to create that happy demeanor and we know instantly when someone is happy or jovial.

By contrast, we also know when someone is sad, feeling down or depressed because we can hear it in the way they deliver the words. My son regularly calls home and has an optimistic outlook, so when he called me one evening and said:

*"Hi Dad, how are you?"* my reply was *"What's wrong?"*

This was because I could tell from a slight sadness or awkwardness in his voice that there was something not quite right. Even though this was the content of his opening call almost every night; I could detect a change in the tone of the voice, which alerted me to an issue.

## U    UNDERSTANDING

The tone and inflection aid in the delivery of the message, but of course the language you use will have a massive bearing on whether the person at the other end of the conversation actually understands what you are saying.

Have you ever had a conversation about something technical, where the person talking to you is using jargon or language that is not normal in your everyday vocabulary and they use a tone and inflection in their voice that suggests that you should understand, and if you don't then you are foolish?

Let me tell you; I have no interest whatsoever in plumbing or what happens to the hot water supply in my house once it leaves my boiler. So on the few occasions where it breaks down all I want from my tradesman is a simple explanation of what's gone wrong, the possible causes and the cost of the repair. A description of valves or the history of how things have changed in the last 20 years is not necessary.

But, like many people I don't want to appear foolish. So my natural reaction when I'm forced to listen to this sort of waffle is to look intently at the person nodding in agreement where I believe it's appropriate. I bow to their superior knowledge in the hope that this friendly acknowledgement may in some way, be reflected in a cheaper price.

When you are having a conversation on the telephone; the situation can become worse as you are unable to pick up on the visual clues that might suggest confusion on behalf of the other party. So it's really important when you are constructing an outbound call that you consider the words and phrases you will use. Keep it appropriate for your audience. If you are calling retail households or businesses then keep the language simple so they understand the content. If you are dealing with counterparts in a similar industry, then it would be fair to assume they will understand some of the technical jargon and abbreviations and it would be sensible to utilise commonly understood terms.

One of the most common mistakes is not having a clear "Call to Action". In other words, what do you want the other person to do or to agree to?

I'm sure you will have seen one of the many TV sitcoms (normally set in large corporate institutions) where a crowd of people gather for yet another meeting, where conversations circle around the room. Everyone wants to contribute in their small way with the latest corporate buzz word, agreeing with each other intently, but without an outcome to the conversation.

Unless the call to action is clear, the conversation will take on an awkward silence and you lose control. If the language or explanation you give to the other person is confusing you may hear the response *"No I'll just leave it thank you!"* This is often polite code for *"I don't understand what you mean"*

**Confusing conversations:  Alice in Wonderland**

**Alice:** Would you tell me, please, which way I ought to go from here?

**The Cat:** That depends a good deal on where you want to get to

**Alice:** I don't much care where.

**The Cat:** Then it doesn't much matter which way you go.

**Alice:** ...so long as I get somewhere.

**The Cat:** Oh, you're sure to do that, if only you walk long enough.

# R    RATE

The rate of speech; the speed at which you talk is another important aspect in the delivery of the message. This is also known as the tempo of the voice and is commonly associated with musical instruments or the singing voice.

When you sing you may follow the instructions on a piece of music and increase (Accelerando) or decrease (Ritardando) the tempo to give the piece meaning or emphasis. With the speaking voice we naturally tend to "Mirror & Match" the person we are speaking to. We explored the power of this rapport building technique earlier and when you are on the telephone, there are two main elements coming into play; the words and the speed of those words.

Imagine you visit an estate agent and say *"Hello; I'm looking for a magnificent property to live in"* The agent, sorts through his files and placing the details in front of you, responds with *"Here's a nice Gaff".* Do you think this will appeal? Of course not.

The second thing is the pace and tempo of the conversation. If you speak too slowly; there is a chance the other person may get bored or frustrated. Speaking too quickly may be difficult for people to understand and the diction may slip causing a loss of meaning.  Regional accents tend to talk at different speeds. In order to have the most impact with your call it is highly likely that you will need to speed up or slow down depending on the area you are calling. It is also a common failing when prospecting by telephone, to rush to get to the end of the call. Having the right flow to the call comes with careful planning and practice so it sounds completely natural to the person listening.

## E    ENTHUSIASM & ENERGY

The enthusiasm in the voice is of course a mixture of tone, pace and inflection and is easily recognisable to the listener and often sums up what they hear (excitement; anticipation; promise; intrigue; suspense; keenness and so forth.)

"Regional accents tend to talk at different speeds. In order to have the most impact with your call it is highly likely that you will need to speed up or slow down depending on the area you are calling. It is also a common failing when prospecting by telephone, to rush to get to the end of the call."

### *"What's wrong with the lot of you?" "It's only a piece of plastic"*

His voice was loud; too loud. He was trying to make his point in a theatrical way; his eyes were wide open and glaring, the perspiration on his receding ginger hairline was sparkling in the florescent light of the classroom. Sam the trainer was in full flow. He was a rounded man in his early forties, no more than 5' 8" in his platform shoes, wearing a grey check suit with a waistcoat to hold in the results of many heavy lunches.

With a strong Glaswegian accent, every word was meticulously spat across the room to his nervous audience. I was in the second row in a room of twenty two hopeful candidates on an induction course for Abbey Life Assurance. I knew there were twenty two, because Sam regularly reminded us that 60% don't pass the induction course and only eight or nine of us would likely see the course through to the end of the week.

Sam was instructing us on the art of "cold calling", the lifeblood of anyone who would be remotely successful in an industry where you only get paid from sales commissions. The audience was silent. I'm not sure this is what I signed up for, to be bullied like a child in a classroom. But then he said something that has stuck with me for the rest of my life.

***"The prospect doesn't know it's your 100th call today..... it's their 1st"***

He made all of us stand up by our telephones (in fact he removed all of the chairs) because he wanted us to project our voices more and to sound more confident when we made the next batch of calls. Sam also explained something else which has served me well over the years. It was a way of dealing with the inevitable "NO" that you would probably receive from 19 out of the next 20 cold calls. He highlighted how much commission we would make on selling a typical product and the sales funnel of activity that was required in order to get to that sale (number of calls, presentations etc.)

It turned out that for every "NO" I received it was worth the equivalent of £10 per call and every "NO" was getting me one closer to the next "YES"

***"So when the next prospect say's NO, Sam barked...put a smile on your face and thank them for their time for they've just earned you £10!"***

Now this may sound very simplistic, but I can assure you it was a turning point for me. Not only did I stand up to project my voice but the physical change in position and attitude in my head meant that my calls carried new meaning and energy.

I became one of the eight! Whilst it wasn't the role for me long-term; it did provide me with invaluable insight and skills that I've used ever since. In this respect far from disliking Sam, I look back on the experience and I am grateful for his guidance.

If your calls lack energy and enthusiasm the prospect will pick up on it immediately; so treat everyone as if it's your first and give them a reason to say YES!

# P.I.C.T.U.R.E.-SUMMARY

- Remember the importance of the first seven seconds

- Practice and listen to your voice. Alter the inflection and tone to give your story maximum effectiveness

- Understand your outcome and have a clear "call to action"

- The prospect doesn't know it's your 100th call...it's the first one to them!

# Chapter Four: Pitch

W e are now ready to start putting together the telephone approach incorporating the Systemised Telephone Elevator Pitch (S.T.E.P ©)

As I explained earlier, there is a big difference between a "Suspect" call and a "Prospect" call. The prospect is someone (company or individual) who at first may have been a "Suspect" and then having discovered that they may have a need for your product or service at some point in the future, become a "Prospect". The **S.T.E.P** © process is designed for the prospect call where you are aiming to talk to the decision maker.

Of course before you get through to the decision maker you will often have to befriend the "gatekeeper." This is a name commonly given to the person who answers the call and is tasked with gathering initial information and filtering calls through to the decision maker. We will examine the best ways to bypass or befriend the "gatekeeper" in a later chapter, so you improve your contact rate with decision makers.

The purpose of the systemised approach is to give you a consistent method and structure to your call so you can

change the message or the content to suit your outcome. In effect you will have a template that works and that can be adapted for almost any sales call.

There are **7 Key Elements** to the call structure:
1. Verification
2. Introduction

3. Green Light
4. Hook
5. Pitch
6. Outcome
7. Response Handling

## Systemised Telephone Elevator Pitch

| | |
|---|---|
| 1. **Verification** | Make sure you are talking to the right person. If you've been put through by the gatekeeper this part may not be necessary. |
| 2. **Introduction** | Remember the instinctive "crocodile brain" will assume the worst, so the prospect has to feel relaxed as soon as possible and believe they are back in control of the call. |
| 3. **Green Light** | The green light is professional and gives you control of the call. It is important to seek permission to continue with the conversation. |

4. **Hook**        The listener will pick up on subject matter that has a bearing to their business or personal circumstances. The crocodile brain will look for things that will surprise it or create intrigue; if this part of the brain is not hooked early in the conversation; it will fail to process further messages to the rest of the brain and they will disengage with the call.

5. **Pitch**       This will be your "Elevator Pitch" reworked into a concise conversational and upbeat few sentences. The purpose of the pitch is to find or create a problem to solve and to create the urgency to take action.

6. **Outcome**     What is your "Call to Action" what do you want to happen as a result of the call?

7. **Response**    If the call has been structured correctly, there will only be a small number of predictable responses and you will have prepared for these.

This is your seven stage template that can be used for the basis of any call. To illustrate how the calls are put together, we will re-visit a couple of the scenarios we created in chapter two.

The first scenario was for the supplier of double glazing units and their target architect customers who would have influence on having their products specified.

In the proposition chapter we created an elevator pitch (below) that would be used when meeting the prospects face to face; now we need to take the key points from this and build it into the **S.T.E.P** © template.

- ✓ You have identified that Mr Smith is a senior partner in a firm of highly respected architects
- ✓ Problems you want to highlight for the prospect are summarised below
- ✓ The solutions that you can provide are also identified
- ✓ The outcome you want to achieve is a face-to-face meeting so you can present your products in a professional manner

*"I'm sure you're aware of the restrictions in glass size currently available in the UK and the fact that if you want something a little bit different to make you stand out; then the lead time has traditionally been a very long."*

*"Of course this means you are competing in the same marketplace with everyone else so you have to work harder to differentiate your company and probably operate on tighter margins to win your fair share of contracts"*

*"We have a state of the art factory here in the UK where we produce the most efficient glass panels in Europe to the latest specifications. Our glass can be produced in much larger sections and we can do that with an extremely quick turnaround from order"*

*"Architects have used our products to create award winning buildings, which has set them apart and allowed them to charge premium prices and to gain preferential status when tendering for new contracts"*

| | |
|---|---|
| **Verification** | ***"Hello Mr Smith; thank you for taking my call"*** |
| **Introduction** | ***"My name is Kevin Charlton; the National Accounts Manager for ABC Glazing Profiles; I'm hoping I'm through to the right person, but if not, perhaps you can point me in the right direction"*** (You have put the prospect in the perceived position of having the power over the call and in doing so relaxed his crocodile brain) |

**Green Light**      *"Are you OK to talk for a moment?"*

**Hook**     *"We have some unique products that have been used on award winning buildings and we work with a number of high profile architect practices like yours"*
(Create the intrigue and position the caller into the same group of organisations)

**Pitch**     *"Because we can offer something a little different, the architects we work with have been able to create buildings that stand out from the crowd and positioned them as the "go to" people for the most prestigious projects"*

*"Naturally that has had a positive effect for them financially and increased their status in the market"*
(In a short paragraph the listener may realise that they are not in the same category and are therefore losing out)

| | |
|---|---|
| **Outcome** | *"So the reason for my call is to arrange a time when I can come and introduce our company, to explain what we can offer, so when you are working on future projects it may influence your approach"* (No immediate push for a sale and therefore less threatening)<br><br>*"I only need about an hour of your time, would later this week or next week be best for you?"* |
| **Response** | We will address the predictable responses in the following chapter. |

The second scenario we created was for our digital marketing company; again the objective will be to get in front of the decision maker, so the process can be replicated from above.

*"We're all aware that the buying habits of customers have changed dramatically in recent years and the Internet is used not only to conduct research of products and services but to interact and to buy online"*

*"This means if companies don't have a joined up approach to digital marketing where they can drive traffic to the site, capture*

*customer details and begin the relationship; they can lose out on thousands of pounds of lost revenue and worse still, project completely the wrong company image"*

*"Our award winning designers are experts in creating the complete package for clients specifically tailored to their business"*

*"Which means you can see measurable improvements in the volume of sales leads that come into your company; reduce the amount you spend on other marketing initiatives and guarantee that when customers look for companies like yours; you stand out"*

## Systemised Telephone Elevator Pitch

| | |
|---|---|
| **Verification** | *"Hello Mr Smith; thank you for taking my call"* |
| **Introduction** | *"My name is Kevin Charlton; the Sales Director for ABC Digital Solutions; I'm hoping I'm through to the right person, but if not, perhaps you can point me in the right direction"* <br> (You have put the prospect in the perceived position of having the power over the call and in doing so relaxed his crocodile brain) |

| | |
|---|---|
| **Green Light** | *"Are you OK to talk for a moment?"* |
| **Hook** | *"You've probably read a recent report from the Chamber of Commerce that identified 87% of companies are losing thousands of pounds every month because they are not handling web based leads effectively"* |

(The prospect may be intrigued by something they've missed. NOTE: this is not a question but a factual statement, because you don't need to have the prospect interrupt at this stage)

| | |
|---|---|
| **Pitch** | *"As you can appreciate, many prospects don't buy on the first visit to your website; in fact the relationship can take some time to nurture and if simple processes and procedures are not in place, you literally throw away business and project a negative image to your customers"* |
| | *"Our clients are able to monitor exactly what's working for them and have increased sales and dramatically cut the costs of their marketing"* |

(Making more money and saving costs are powerful drivers)

**Outcome** *"At this stage; I have no way of knowing if you fall into the 13% of companies that are doing a great job; so if I could take an hour of your time; I will quickly be able to assess the situation and show you your options for creating more business. Would you be free later this week or is next week best?"* (Always use the alternative close)

**Response** We will address the predictable responses in the following chapter.

You can see the technique employed and they are designed for similar outcomes (the face-to-face meeting); but what if you wanted a different outcome; to make a sale over the telephone for example?

Imagine you work for a company selling wine and you've been given sales leads of people that have indicated an interest in wine; maybe as part of a joint promotion when they bought a book online. Clearly the person you are about to call is not a customer but does fall into the category of "Prospect". The purpose of the call will be to start the relationship and to sell this prospect the introductory case of wine and to create a lasting relationship.

Typically, this type of prospect may buy wine at a local merchant or supermarket. They perhaps buy the wine on offer with a perceived saving and often it is the same wine that their friends may buy from the same places. There is something quite nice about being made to feel special, especially if you can then talk to others about the quality of the wine, knowing you've had a great buying experience.

This type of call may turn into something more conversational and take longer, but nevertheless you still follow the template to build value and to hook the prospect. The "Call to Action" will be to take credit card details. The call may be something like:

> "This type of call may turn into something more conversational and take longer, but nevertheless you still follow the template to build value and to hook the prospect. The "Call to Action" will be to take credit card details."

## Systemised Telephone Elevator Pitch

**Verification**     *"Hello is that Mr Smith?"*

**Introduction**     *"It's only Kevin Charlton from ABC Specialist Wines; you recently purchased from one of our trading partners and you indicated that you enjoy a glass of fine wine from time to time"*
(The word "Only" has the effect of lowering the risk of the call)

**Green Light**     *"Are you OK to talk for a moment?"*

**Hook**     *"If it's OK with you I would just like to have a quick chat to see if you qualify to be one of our "Platinum Members" and to receive significant savings on world class wines"*
(This may cause the intrigue in the crocodile brain as to why they may not qualify)

**Pitch**

*"Most of our members previously bought wine from local merchants or supermarkets and they found either they had a limited choice, or for something a bit special; they would pay a much higher price"*

*"We have been specialists in wine for 40 years and our buyers have incredible relationships with vineyards throughout the world. We find unique wines, generally of a much higher quality and we are able to work closely with the wine producers so we obtain fantastic wholesale prices"*

*"We tailor offers for our members so they tend to stay with us for a long time and provide us with outstanding testimonials, which is how we have been able to grow our business"*

*"So can I ask you a few questions about what you like?"*
(Membership appeals to a lot of people and by qualifying their buying habits it gives the prospect a say in proceedings)

**Outcome**    *"Well you are certainly eligible to be a member and as such we can offer you our outstanding introductory case of your chosen wines at half price. This means most bottles are much cheaper than even supermarket prices"*

*"In addition there is also a 100% money back guarantee on any of the wines that you did not feel were suitable and no membership fees so you are not tied into any ongoing cases"*

*"If you are happy to become a member I can help you select your case now and all I need is a credit card number"*

(The 100% money back guarantee is the "Puppy Dog" close I mentioned in an earlier chapter removing the risk from the decision)

**Response**    We will address the predictable responses in the following chapter.

So as you can see, regardless of the type of call, you can follow the structure of **S.T.E.P.** © to create order and add clarity to the call. Does this mean that you always achieve your outcome...of course not; but the system will provide you with a consistent approach and this in turn builds confidence. A confident caller is generally more productive.

*"Confidence comes from discipline and training"*
**Robert Kiyosaki**

# PITCH - SUMMARY

- The system works for any call; simply fill out the blanks

- Be aware of the "Crocodile Brain" and get ready to intrigue

- Pick out the key emotive words and keep it short and concise

- Understand your "Call to Action"

- Delivery of the story in everything!

# Chapter Five: Predictable Responses

There is nothing more frustrating in sales than the prospect saying "no" to your offer. Rejection is a very basic trigger that creates negative emotions, predominantly one of fear. We all fear losing things:

- Losing our health
- Losing our life
- Losing our status
- Losing our peace of mind
- Losing money
- Losing our youth and looks

We also fear, perhaps more than anything else, losing approval from others. Fear of rejection is widespread. In tribal times, being ejected from the safety of a group could have meant death. No wonder many of us like to 'fit in'.

You see this in children when they are forced to move schools frequently because parents have work commitments elsewhere. They are desperate to fit in and it can be traumatic for them to integrate with other children who already have their circles of friends.

When face to face with a prospect, rejection is slightly easier to deal with for most salespeople, because they have the opportunity to use all of the visual clues and body language to counter the knock back. On the telephone, when you are selling or attempting to set up a meeting, you are reliant upon your persuasive storytelling and the enthusiasm in your voice to overcome their negative response.

I completely understand the fear that most people in business or sales have in making telephone calls. When I coach people on telephone techniques I always start with the potential reasons for not wanting to make a call and produce a list of their concerns. Here are some of the common responses I receive:

- *"It's a waste of time"*
- *"I'm much better face to face"*
- *"I prefer to go out on pre-arranged appointments"*
- *"The results are rubbish for all the effort you put in"*
- *"The quality of the leads is really poor"*
- *"If they wanted to buy they would have contacted us"*
- *"We haven't got anything good to offer"*
- *"I tried it once before and it didn't work"*
- *"I hate receiving calls when I'm at home"*
- *"I don't know what to say"*
- *"I can't handle the customers objections"*
- *"My time is better spent selling not prospecting"*
- *"It's not the right time to call"*
- *"We should send out letters before we call"*

I could probably think of many more, but if the response is drilled down the final reason that invariably unfolds is: **"I don't like the rejection"**

This is the BIG one. The others are simply excuses to avoid making the calls because ultimately they don't want to feel the rejection. The purpose of this book is to provide a template and develop techniques in order that callers can maximise their chances of success. Does this mean that everyone will roll over and give you an appointment or buy your products; definitely not. But remember the phrase used in sales: *"Some will. Some won't. So what."*

It's really important to realise that most people don't mean "No Never" they mean No, "Not Now" or No, "I Don't Understand"

In John Fenton's book (*Close Close Close*) he discusses a piece of international research known as the 8/73 Survey. This was a study of how salespeople reacted to objections from customers. In the context of the report the "No's" are classified as "No, not yet". In other words the prospect still has some doubts over the sale and hasn't yet reached a conclusion. It suggests that further attempts at communication should be attempted but the survey showed:

- 44% of salespeople gave up after receiving the first objection
- 22% of salespeople gave up after receiving the second objection

- 16% of salespeople gave up after receiving the third objection
- 10% of salespeople gave up after receiving the fourth objection

If you add up the number of people who have given up after receiving 4 objections it is 92%. So this only leaves 8% of salespeople still selling. That's the 8 part of the 8/73 survey.

The second part of the survey was research based on customer objections. The reasons for the objections were varied but 73% would give five or more of them before agreeing to an order. So the 8% of salespeople who keep going will win 73% of the business.

Now this is all very good and when I read the book I understood the importance of being persistent; but that didn't help me when I had no idea of what to say to overcome the objections.

I recall when I was selling cars in a retail environment. We were taught a process for qualifying the customer and presenting the right car to them. After demonstrating the car we would present a figure for the customer to buy.

Nobody taught me how to ask for the order. Inevitably some customers simply had some doubts that I'd not covered off and would give me the phrase *"OK let me go and think about it, I never make a decision on the day"*

My objection handling technique was pitiful and I would say *"Are you sure? Nothing else I can do today?"*

I would then agree to call them the next day...and it got worse! I would ring and ask them *"Any more thoughts?"* This, of course, 90% of the time got another negative response.

Hindsight and experience are wonderful and what I should have said on the follow up call was: *"I know you wanted some time to think about it...hopefully you still like the car as much as you did yesterday, so the reason for my call is to get your deposit"* At least this would get a real objection or a credit card number.

Having made literally thousands of sales calls both business to consumer and business to business, I realised that there are only **6 possible responses** to your initial call and only three of them really matter once you have the prospect showing an interest in your offer. (Please note I am talking about "Prospect" calls and not "Suspect" calls.) This was a breakthrough moment because I was able to fashion a technique to deal with the six objection types.

You can remember the six with the acronym **WATMAN**©

| | |
|---|---|
| **WHO** | Who are you? |
| **AUTHORITY** | It's not me who makes the decisions |
| **TIME** | I don't have time to talk to you |

| **MONEY** | We don't have any money to spend |
| **ALTERNATIVE** | We use an alternative provider |
| **NEED** | I don't see the need for your offer |

On the basis that these responses are not necessarily real objections, all we have to do is consider what they are really seeking.

## WHO

This is a request for further information about you or your organisation so the prospect can make a decision about whether the call may be relevant.

## AUTHORITY

The prospect understands what the call is about but needs to refer you to someone else who has the authority to make decisions.

## TIME

The prospect is giving you the chance to arrange a more convenient time for the discussion.

## MONEY

At this stage the prospect does not know if there is a cost attached to what you want to talk about or indeed how it may save them money

**ALTERNATIVE**

On the basis that the prospect uses an alternative provider, it demonstrates that they have a need for your type of offer.

**NEED**

This may be a lack of understanding about what you can offer at this stage .

## TRIPLE "R"© Response Handling

Because all prospect's responses are predictable and known; I developed a method of dealing with them in a friendly and professional manner; I refer to it as the **TRIPLE "R"** process. Having a process or technique creates confidence. The phrase *"Repetition is the Mother of Skill"* comes to mind, because the more times you do something the easier it becomes. It's muscle memory, just like playing the piano or delivering the perfect golf swing, the practice and repetition turn it into an unconscious behaviour.

There are also bad practices by some organisations, when they attempt to create a predictable response. I received a call recently from a call centre trying to gain my interest in installing solar panels. The call started badly as there was a pause after I answered, either because the caller was dialing "hands free" and was slow to pick up, or I was one of many potential customers on speed dial where they only click into the call if there is a prospect response.

The caller made a mistake with my name (apparently Mr Chilten was also on their list to call!) and then he proceeded down a scripted approach that demonstrated a lack of any real interest.

*"Mr Charlton my name is Mike from North Western Alternative Energy. You may be aware of the Government's drive to push for alternative green energy solutions and at North Western we have the most advanced solar panels which we are fitting to thousands of homes"*

NOTICE: there was no "Green Light" to find out if I had time to talk.

*"Would you be interested in saving money on your household energy bills?"*

As you know from an earlier chapter, this is a closed question and destined to get a yes or no response. Presumably, when designing their approach, the company were hoping that most people would say yes, which would allow the caller to continue to explain how they could meet this need. Of course when you ask a closed question, there's a 50 / 50 chance of the response being negative. This is where the company's response handling was ill prepared and almost confrontational.

*"No I'm not interested thank you"*

*"What! You're not interested in saving money?"*

It is essential when designing any outbound call, that you follow the **S.T.E.P.** © approach and consider the outcome you want to receive.

## TRIPLE "R"©

**R**EPEAT
Repeat the response back to the prospect so they know that you've listened

**R**E-POSITION
Actively listen to the response and re-position the discussion with a counter argument

**R**E-DIRECT
Move them towards the outcome you want to achieve

If the technique is utilised and practiced it becomes like a drill in the head of the caller; it is not confrontational and in many cases will enable you to achieve your outcome or, at least, uncover the real objection.

To demonstrate how **TRIPLE "R"** can be utilised, we will go back to one of our earlier examples in the **S.T.E.P.** process; ABC Glazing Profiles, where the caller was attempting to gain face-to-face meeting with the decision maker.

| | |
|---|---|
| **Verification** | *"Hello Mr Smith; thank you for taking my call"* |
| **Introduction** | *"My name is Kevin Charlton; the National Accounts Manager for ABC Glazing Profiles; I'm hoping I'm through to the right person, but if not, perhaps you can point me in the right direction"* |
| **Green Light** | *"Are you OK to talk for a moment?"* |
| **Hook** | *"We have some unique products that have been used on award winning buildings and we work with a number of high profile architect practices like yours"* |

| | |
|---|---|
| **Pitch** | *"Because we can offer something a little different, the architects we work with have been able to create buildings that stand out from the crowd and positioned them as the "go to" people for the most prestigious projects"* |
| | *"Naturally this has had a positive effect for them financially and increased their status in the market"* |
| **Outcome** | *"So the reason for my call is to arrange a time when I can come and introduce our company, to explain what we can offer, so when you are working on future projects it may influence your approach"* *"I only need about an hour of your time, would later this week or next week be best for you?"* |

Decision Makers initial response: **WHO**

*"I haven't actually come across your company; why don't you put some information in the post"*

**R**EPEAT            *"I understand that you may not have heard about us; we tend to gain a lot of referrals and as such we don't find the need to advertise too heavily"*

**R**E-POSITION       *"I would be happy to put something in the post, but much of what we do is bespoke to our clients which has enabled them to win high profile contracts"*

**R**E-DIRECT         *"At this stage, I only need an hour of your time so I can leave you with all the information, so when you are ready to consider a specific project; then maybe we can be of assistance. Are you free later this week or is next week best for you?"*

Remember, the purpose of the technique is to push past what may be a perceived objection and to re-direct the prospect back to your outcome and in doing so always use an "Alternative" close so the prospect is more likely to pick one of your two choices. Do not slip into *"When is good for you?"* because you lose control of the appointment.

Decision Makers initial response: **AUTHORITY**

**"I'm sorry but it's not me that you need to talk to"**

| | |
|---|---|
| **R**EPEAT | *"OK I understand"* |
| **R**E-POSITION | *"Who is the best person to contact?"* |
| **R**E-DIRECT | *"Can you put me through?"* |

Decision Makers initial response: **TIME**

**"I'm really too busy at the moment, we have a lot on"**

| | |
|---|---|
| **R**EPEAT | *"Well it's great that you are busy"* |
| **R**E-POSITION | *"What we have to offer could make a big difference to the way in which you operate and the sort of projects you can win. So it's important for both of us that we can put some quality time aside"* |
| **R**E-DIRECT | *"I will only need an hour of your time to introduce you to what we do; how is your diary looking later this month perhaps 25th or 26th?"* |

Decision Makers initial response: **MONEY**

**"We can't look at fresh ideas at the moment; we are working to really tight budgets"**

**R**EPEAT

*"I completely understand how important it is to be careful when it comes to budgeting"*

**R**E-POSITION

*"We offer a range of solutions that could make you more competitive or position you to win higher value contracts"*

**R**E-DIRECT

*"I will only need an hour of your time to introduce you to what we do; how is your diary looking later this week or early next week?"*

Decision Makers initial response: **ALTERNATIVE**

*"We already work with companies like yours offering tailored solutions"*

**R**EPEAT                    *"That's great; clearly you can see the benefits these relationships may bring"*

**R**E-POSITION               *"Quite often what we have to offer compliments existing arrangements and can add even more value to your projects"*

**R**E-DIRECT                 *"I will only need an hour of your time to introduce you to what we do; how is your diary looking later this week or early next week?"*

Decision Makers initial response: **NEED**

**"I don't think we really have the need for such a service"**

**R**EPEAT                    *"I understand; several other clients thought the same thing in the early stages"*

**R**E-POSITION               *"Once they had the opportunity to see what we had to offer and how we were able to help them differentiate themselves from their competitors; they were delighted"*

RE-DIRECT

*"I will only need an hour of your time to introduce you to what we do; how is your diary looking later this week or early next week?"*

## It's a drill!

13th October 2009; three minutes into injury time with Greece leading England 2-1 and England about to crash out of the World Cup; a free kick is awarded 30 yards from the Greek goal.

A capacity crowd at Old Trafford fell silent as Captain David Beckham placed the ball. This was the last possible chance for England to draw the match and secure a place in the finals in South Africa. The whistle blew and a nation held its breath.

It was the most unbelievable strike; the ball, bent and twisted in the air and curled into the top right hand corner of the goal. The goalkeeper moved one way then the other but was left flat footed, staring in disbelief as the ball bulged the net. The crowd and everyone watching at home screamed; seconds before the final whistle David Beckham wrote his name in football history and saved the nation from the embarrassment of World Cup elimination.

Was it a lucky strike? No. David Beckham would never be regarded as a world class player; but he was world class when it came to taking free kicks. He knew his limitations as a footballer; he did not have lightening pace or the ability to dribble past people; so he perfected his ability to bend the ball around defenders with uncanny accuracy so forwards could be guaranteed a shot on target.

The skill was developed with hours of practice. He would remain on the training ground for another 30-40 minutes after the rest of the team had left the field. With a bag of balls he would pepper the goal from all angles so he knew the optimum run up and exactly how to shape his foot for the strike.

If you are going to be really successful at anything, it takes practice; and if your livelihood is determined by how many sales you make or appointments gained by telephone; practice is essential.

Don't practice on potential customers, find a friend or a colleague and practice with them. Remember you only get one chance to make a first impression!

# PREDICTABLE RESPONSES – SUMMARY

- There are only 6 responses and only 3 once you've made your presentation

- No rarely means "No Never"

- Remember the 8/73 survey and be one of the 8%

- Your objective is to find the real objection... if it exists!

- Practice makes perfect

# Chapter 6: Selling at the Top

For more years than I care to remember, I wasted my time selling to the wrong level within the organisations I approached. This may be familiar to you, if you are in business to business sales.

IBM was once one of the most respected companies in the world, with an enviable record of having some of the most respected and high profile sales people. But the world changed and sales began to tumble; IBM commissioned a survey to discover two things:

1.  The skills most critical for business in selling products or services. These involved:

    a.  Big money
    b.  Multiple decision makers
    c.  Long sales cycles
    d.  Top management approval
    e.  An ongoing relationship

2. IBM's level of performance of the most critical skills

Here is the ranking of the five skills that were found to be the most critical for success, yet the lowest in the level of performance:

1. Calling at the top
2. Consultative skills
3. Listening skills
4. Influencing skills
5. Questioning skills

When I stumbled across this survey, it was a lightbulb moment for me.

When I considered why I hadn't been selling at the top, I had to admit to two things:

1. I hadn't considered what I might talk about
2. I didn't feel comfortable calling at that level

At the time I was probably making 10 fresh sales calls a week so let's say 500 calls a year. So how many sales techniques was I using every year? That's right, just one!

On the other hand if I was the buyer in an organisation and I received 2 sales pitches a day, that's also 500 a year. How many selling techniques would the customer see? The answer is many different ones; so it was time for me to be different. I would sell to the top.

In my early days selling training solutions I would establish from the "Gatekeeper" (more about them shortly) who, in the organisation, was responsible for training. Having completed my "Suspect" call, the company had now turned into a genuine prospect and I proceeded to chase down my new found target. Typically, the following scenario would unfold:

- I may make 4-5 telephone calls to get through to the prospect

- After initial knock backs, the prospect would agree to meet with me
- During the meeting I would uncover sufficient problems in order to present my training solution
- The prospect would insist that their company was different and a more tailored solution would be necessary
- I would agree to do some initial research (free of charge) analysing their specific requirements
- A second meeting would be agreed but not normally for a few weeks, because my prospect would be busy
- At the second meeting I would present my tailored solution. Let's assume I have a 50 /50 chance of gaining acceptance and the prospect wants a formal written proposal so he / she could take it to the board... because they don't have the authority to sign off on the deal.
- Now I am reliant upon someone else gaining me an appointment to present to the real decision maker and several weeks have now passed
- Finally I present to the board and again let's assume there is a 50 /50 chance of acceptance. So this is a 50/50 decision on top of the 50/50 chance of getting this far (25% overall)
- This maybe one of the most important business decisions the board will consider this year, so it is not unreasonable to assume they will want to consider other vendors. Let's say I win 50% of the time but this makes my overall success rate now 12.5% and probably 6-8 weeks of my time has been invested in this.

So the golden rule is to sell at the top; they are very rarely 9 feet tall giants who breathe fire; actually they are normally really easy people to deal with. They will let you know up-front if you are wasting your time. They are better placed to describe the decision making criteria and where you stand and they are in a superior position to cascade authority down the hierarchy of the organisation.

The fact of the matter is when you sell at the top; there is a better understanding of value and less reliance upon price. When you sell at the top there is always less competition.

## The Rule of Common Sense
## – John Ruskin (1819-1900)

"It's unwise to pay too much, but it's worse to pay too little. When you pay too much, you lose a little money....that's all. When you pay too little, you sometimes lose everything, because the thing you bought was incapable of doing the thing it was bought to do.

The common law of business balance prohibits paying a little and getting a lot...it can't be done.

If you deal with the lowest bidder, it is well to add something for the risk you run, and if you do that you will have enough to pay for something better"

# SELLING AT THE TOP – SUMMARY

- It will save you time and money

- They are just as human as you and will appreciate a good call

- They appreciate value are less fixated on cost

- If they are not the decision maker, authority flows better downhill!

# Chapter Seven: Gatekeepers

Over the years I have read so many articles and techniques on "How to bypass the gatekeeper" and frankly, most of them make me sick!

First of all, let me explain the metaphorical use that has been given to the term "Gatekeeper".

Historically a "Gatekeeper" would be a human who controls access to something; such as the gates to a City. In the late 20th century the title was bestowed upon anyone controlling the access to information or to protecting others within the organisation from outsiders.

Typically these "Gatekeepers" are personal assistants; secretaries; junior managers or even spouses & partners in small businesses. Their role is to filter enquiries and to decipher what information to pass on, or who to allow through to the decision maker. Without this filtering process, decision makers would be handling a multitude of irrelevant calls and making decisions, perhaps more suited to others in the organisation. Let's face it; we all rely on these filters. How many times have you heard the phrase;

or indeed used it yourself: ***"Would you just take a message for me?"***

Gatekeepers are just doing their job....so please respect them!

So many sales trainers and business coaches advocate that "gatekeepers" are the enemy and to treat them in a subordinate manner; because what the caller has to discuss with the decision maker is far too important for them!

Imagine if you were the gatekeeper, or indeed your gatekeeper was involved with this conversation:

| | |
|---|---|
| Gatekeeper: | Ms. Jones office; Mike Smith speaking; how can I help you? |
| Prospect: | Ms. Jones, please. |
| Gatekeeper: | May I ask who's calling? |
| Prospect: | Bill Cartwright from ABC media. |
| Gatekeeper: | And what's it in connection with Mr Cartwright? |
| Prospect: | I just need a quick word, because I want to arrange a meeting. |

Gatekeeper:     OK well I organise Ms. Jones' diary but before she will agree to a time I need to understand what the meeting will be about.

Prospect:     Listen. You wouldn't understand, but trust me when I say; it will be worth her while!

Gatekeeper:     Can I suggest that you send me details of the content of the meeting by e-mail and I will make sure that Ms. Jones reads it. Then, if appropriate, we can come back to you with potential dates and time for a meeting? Would you like my e-mail details?

Prospect:     It's not something that can easily be explained in an e-mail all I need is 30 minutes of her time; I'm sure you wouldn't want her to miss out on a great opportunity so is she free tomorrow afternoon?

You can see where this conversation will end up. Do not underestimate the power of the "gatekeeper" there is a very good chance that they completely understand the character of the decision maker and they are held in high esteem by them. Alienating or irritating them will not be profitable.

Let's think of it in a different way. Without any prior knowledge of their occupation or role in life; the same individuals meet in different circumstances, perhaps at a social gathering; can you acknowledge the difference in the appreciation for each other?

Bill Cartwright:   Hi, I'm Bill

Mike Smith:   Nice to meet you; I'm Mike.

Bill:   So, what is it you do for a living?

Mike:   I'm the personal assistant to the editor of XYZ Highlife. And you?

Bill:   I work in advertising. So what brought you to the party? Who do you know here?

Mike:   Just a friend of a friend. Did you see the match last night?

Why is it that your natural character, displayed in social circumstances and one that you are comfortable with, will turn into something very different in business? Be natural...it will always shine through!

My view and something that has always worked well for me, is to ensure you befriend the gatekeeper and get them onside. After all you will undoubtedly have several conversations to get to the decision maker and hopefully a lot more in the future when they become a valuable client.

Throughout, be honest and use integrity. Make it personal and always respect their position. At the same time do not come across as timid or inferior; you need confidence and authority in your voice and overall be prepared for the "predictable responses" so you have your **TRIPLE "R"** © objection handling responses ready. Take several deep breaths and breathe out through the nose to calm yourself and smile as you connect with the caller because these emotions will transfer down the line.

Let's take another look at Bill Cartwright's call from a different approach.

| | |
|---|---|
| Gatekeeper: | **Ms. Jones office; Mike Smith speaking; how can I help you?** |
| Prospect: | **Hello Mike; I'm calling for Ms. Jones.** *(By acknowledging the PA's name, you have already given them respect. I've always found this to be slightly more personal and successful)* |
| Gatekeeper: | **May I ask who's calling?** |

Prospect: **Of course, it's Bill Cartwright from ABC media.**

Gatekeeper: **And what's it in connection with Mr Cartwright?**

Prospect: **Well, perhaps this is where you can help me. I would like to arrange a 30 minute meeting to discuss something that may be of interest to her; do you look after her diary, in which case I don't need to speak to her at this stage?** *(You have asked for help and remember the law of reciprocity. Of course all we want at this stage is a face to face meeting so getting through to the decision maker at this stage may be counter-productive)*

Gatekeeper: **OK. Well I do organise Ms. Jones' diary but before she will agree to a time I need to understand what the meeting will be about.**

Prospect: **I understand, but it's a little complicated to explain over the telephone. However, we have some ideas that could dramatically increase sales revenues and cut costs. As I say I only need 30 minutes of her time at this stage so she can make an informed decision, so when do you think would be good for her, later this week or next week?** *(Of course we do not want to discuss the details but giving some clear benefits for the meeting may help. Only 30 minutes is a disarming phrase and you are giving the power back to the potential client in making the final decisions. Taking control of the gatekeeper by suggesting one of two dates often gets them thinking of the appointment rather than another objection)*

Gatekeeper: **Can I suggest that you send me details of the content of the meeting by e-mail and I will make sure that Ms. Jones reads it; then, if appropriate, we can come back to you with potential dates and time for a meeting? Would you like my e-mail details?**

| | |
|---|---|
| Prospect: | **I would love your e-mail details, because then I can keep you in the loop and I will provide you with a brief overview; but as I said it really will take a brief meeting for Ms. Jones to understand what we can offer. So can we schedule a date and time now; I will send you an e-mail and if there's problem you can come back to me.** *(Once again you have given them respect and succumbed to his request; of course the e-mail will be suitably vague and you've pressed for the appointment. Offering to keep him in the loop will more than likely lead to an appointment)* |

Keeping it personal also means sending a personalised note, e-mail or handwritten, thanking the gatekeeper for their help....this goes a long way!

## GATEKEEPERS – SUMMARY

- Gatekeepers can be your "Best Friend" or your "Worst Enemy"

- Never underestimate the power of the gatekeeper

- Make them feel they are involved, but do not pitch to them as they rarely have authority in the decision making process

- Send them a note to thank them for their help

- Where possible use their name

# Chapter Eight:
# Measure & Monitor

You've probably heard the phrase *"If you don't measure; you can't manage"* and this is particularly true in sales.

I was rudely made aware of this when selling life assurance on a commission only basis. I mentioned earlier about my torrid time with the sales trainer, educating me to make cold calls. During the same induction week, he explained about measuring sales activity; a fact that must have slipped me by when I actually started selling.

One of the key principles of selling life assurance was to build a network of clients that you could service and the most successful way of finding new people was to ask for referrals from clients that you had just sold to. This was quite a pressure and potentially uncomfortable for the salesperson and particularly the new client. This is how the situation would pan out:

Having spent several hours with a young couple in their home, often at 9:00 pm you would shake hands on the

completion of products and services you would provide. Having gained their trust and built outstanding rapport you were then trained to say:

*"Thank you both for that, I'm glad you are comfortable with your decision. Now as you can appreciate, I gain most of my business through satisfied clients and the friends and family members they can introduce me to."*

*"So thinking about your close circle of friends and family, can you give me six names and telephone numbers of people that I could contact so I can introduce myself?"*

The trick was then to completely shut up; look the client in the eye and hold your pen over the referral section of your fact find, very confidently expecting them to blurt out names and numbers.

In reality, it was far more challenging. They would be hesitant, not wanting to push me onto others that may feel offended with my approach.

*"I'm not sure we would like to do that, at least not before calling them first"*

*"I understand but you will recall that I was given your details from your work colleague John and all I want to do is exactly what I've done with you and find out if there is anything I can help them with moving forward. You know*

*I haven't been pushy in anyway with you; I simply want to introduce myself even if that is for a future time; so who can you think of?"*

Because I stuck to the trained techniques, this became very successful for me and I discovered that when I phoned these referrals, I would gain an appointment rate of about 50%. Then after meeting with them I would close about 50% of them into a sale. The leads I obtained as referrals were far superior to any cold calls I made and very soon I was one of the most successful members of the team.

This is when I became too confident and my process began to change. I mentioned about the importance of a process earlier on. Instead of insisting on six names and numbers from new clients, I began to ease up the pressure I put onto them and asked for "A Couple" of names and numbers I could contact. I still had the same appointment rate from my telephone calls and I still sold to half of the appointments. The problem was, after another month or so I couldn't make my mortgage payments.

This was as a direct result of changing my process, but at the same time my ratios for sales conversions still remained as strong...a sobering lesson with a young family to feed!

There are several numbers that you must be aware of, if you are going to plan to succeed!

Generally, in business to business sales there are a number of stages to measure and monitor.

1. **What is your success rate from final presentation to sale?** In other words you are presenting your proposal / solution to the person who can make a decision; how many times out of 10 would they buy? If this is 2 out of 10 then it's 20% if it is 8 out of 10, 80%

2. **How many fact find meetings do you need to get to final presentations?** This is the number of initial meetings you have with someone who has an interest in your offer and the percentage of them who decide it is worth taking through to a full presentation. So if you get in front of 10 decision makers and 5 of them agree there is some merit in your proposal and they ask you to come back with figures, then it's 50%

3. **How many appointments do you make from decision maker telephone conversations?** This is the measure of the number of conversations you have with decision makers over the telephone who then agree to meet with you. So if you contact 20 decision makers and 8 agree to an initial meeting, it will be 40%

4. **What is the contact rate through to decision makers from prospect calls?** In other words, how many calls do I have to make in order to get through

to the person who can grant me a meeting or a sale? So if you attempt to ring 50 prospects and you only manage to talk to 10 decision makers then that is 20%

5. **There is also the measure of how many calls you need to make in order to find a prospect.** But for the purposes of this section, we will discuss the ratios from prospects.

Obviously the conversions at each stage will vary greatly depending on the industry and the quality of the salesperson; but we will assume the following:

- **For every final presentation made you have a 70% conversion to sale**
  Consider for a moment how many sales you need in a period for survival. For arguments sake, let's say that's 10. In order to reach the 10 you need to make **14** final presentations to the decision maker.

- **80% of fact-find initial meetings will result in a final presentation**
  The stage before a final presentation is often referred to as the fact find meeting. During this meeting you will discover if there is an opportunity to move to the final presentation. It is unlikely that this will always be 100%.In order to achieve the 14 final presentations you will have to conduct **18** fact find meetings.

- **Appointment rate from decision maker contact to fact find meeting is 50%**
  When you speak to the decision maker on the telephone, there will be a number who are simply not interested in meeting with you. On the basis that this is 50% you will have to contact **36** decision makers on the telephone.

- **You have a success rate from prospect calls to decision maker conversations of 60%**
  In order to generate 36 conversations with decision makers based upon a contact rate of 60% you will need to make **60** telephone prospect calls. (see the diagram below)

| Activity | Outcome |
| --- | --- |
| 60 prospect calls | |
| 60% success rate in getting through to the decision maker | 36 conversations with Decision Makers |
| 36 decision maker conversations with 50% success in gaining a fact find appointment | 18 face-to-face appointments with Decision Makers |

| | |
|---|---|
| 80% success rate in creating sufficient interest to get to presentation stage | 14 presentations to the Decision Maker |
| 70% success rate in selling from presentation | 10 sales completed |

One of the things that I struggled with in my early years as a salesman was to calculate the level of activity required at the beginning of the month in order to hit target, based on my usual success rates.

Sometimes I have to work with clients to explain the importance of knowing these numbers and indeed how to back-calculate the numbers so they can see the level of sales activity at each stage in the process. To illustrate this perhaps the diagram of the sales funnel will make it easier to understand.

Let's also assume you want to make 10 sales in the period.

## SALES ACTIVITY FUNNEL

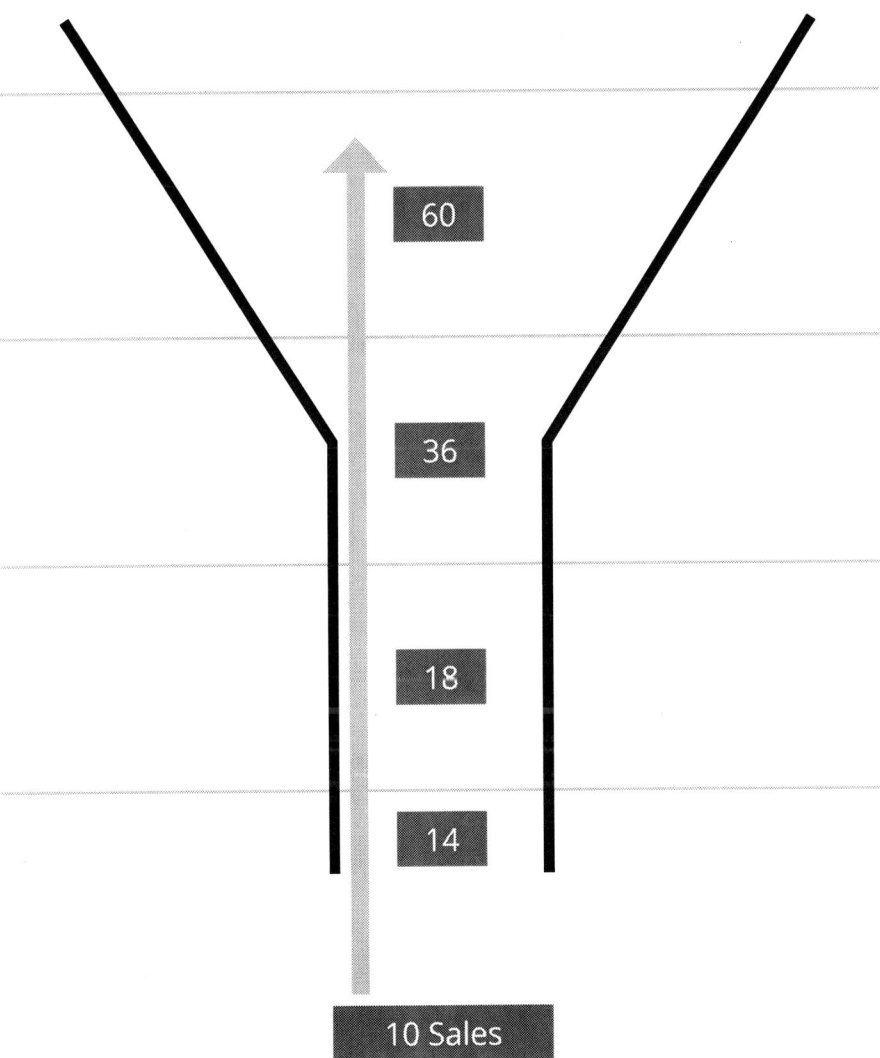

So you can see that the measurement at each stage of the process is very important, but so too is the monitoring and analysis of information, because this will tell you where you can improve your approach or techniques.

- If your close rate from final presentations is low for your industry (and this will depend on industry, because selling cars is very different to selling tanks) then you need to consider how well your solution eliminates the problem; how well you made your case and did you ask for the business...remember **B.E.V.A.**

## B.E.V.A. Benefit Emotion Value Ask

- If you have met a decision maker but you are experiencing difficulties in getting from the initial fact-find meeting to another presentation appointment, then you should consider:

  o Your ability to qualify and uncover potential problems
  o Were you presenting too soon, rather than listening and gathering information
  o Look at the appeal of your offer and does it differ sufficiently from the competition

- Having achieved a telephone conversation with the decision maker, how likely are you to succeed at gaining that all important face to face meeting?

  o Are you delivering your WHAT and not your WHY?
  o Have you told them too much so they don't need to see you?

- o Have you completed your "Homework" before the call?
- o Analyse the quality of your delivery; did it sound convincing and were you prepared for initial knock backs?

- If you are having to make too many calls to speak to a decision maker:

  - o What is the quality of the **S.T.E.P** © process?
  - o Are you selling at the top?
  - o What is your relationship like with the "gatekeeper"?
  - o Consider your **PITCH** and make it more punchy
  - o Practice the delivery and think of every element of **P.I.C.T.U.R.E**
  - o Do you need to re-visit **W.A.T.M.A.N.**© and **TRIPLE "R"**©
  - o Are you persistent and disciplined enough with the time you allocate to making these calls?
  - o Are you calling at the right time of day (in the building industry I would often get into the office early and call contractors at about eight o'clock. PA's and secretaries rarely started this early and the decision makers regularly answered the phone!)
  - o If you do decide to leave answerphone messages, do not tell the whole story and leave yourself in control of the next action. ***"Hi It's only...(me)...I have some great news....but don't worry I'll call you another time"*** (Create intrigue and alert the crocodile brain!)

Success in any business is dependent upon attracting sufficient sales. All too often we look around to find other excuses as to why we are failing to achieve potential. (The market is bad; people aren't making decisions; the weather is having an effect; my new employees are just learning; it's just that time of year etc.)

Sometimes it is easy to hide behind these excuses, especially in larger organisations where people become less accountable; but if you are a sole trader or small business and your livelihood depends on daily sales activity; you cannot ignore the basic facts. If you are a manager in a large organisation and you are encountering similar results; then you must examine the symptoms!

If you stand still you are not changing and evolving and the net result is you are going backwards. Others around you are innovating and coming up with a better product than yours or finding a different way to solve people's problems.

"Success in any business is dependent upon attracting sufficient sales. All too often we look around to find other excuses as to why we are failing to achieve potential."

Do not become an IBM. Keep monitoring the success at every stage in the process so you know if your sales pitch (initially over the telephone) is becoming stale, if it is, **then change it!** Think of another way of presenting the same information or creating intrigue.

Benjamin Franklin once said: ***"If you fail to plan, you are planning to fail!"*** I cannot think of a better quote so I won't attempt one! Change happens quickly in every business environment. If you are completely aligned with your sales approach over the telephone and it is current and vibrant; then you will succeed over your competition.

# MEASURE & MONITOR – SUMMARY

- If you don't measure you can't manage

- Measure sales activity as well as the result

- Examine performance at each stage of the process to identify specific areas for improvement

- Shortcutting the process will detrimentally affect the outcome, there are steps in the process for a reason

- Plan to succeed at the beginning of each period and monitor outcomes regularly

- If the goal was realistic and you find yourself failing...change the approach, not the goal

# Chapter Nine: A Final Story

## The best stories originate from real situations.

In an attempt to summarise the contents of this book, I thought it appropriate to re-visit the time when I first realised that I had a successful process and a SYSTEM I could adopt to help me (and others) become more successful at using the telephone.

As you may have gathered, my sales experience covers many different spheres and each one has taught me a thing or two about adapting my process and approach.

Early in my sales career, I'd been appointed as one of 12 recruits from outside the retail motor industry to work in a business to business selling role for a prestige car brand and my role would be to promote the marque to local businesses in my area.

The training was intensive and to be honest I was a little in awe of the trainers and the volume of information thrust upon us. We were treated very well, the best hotels and dining, trips abroad and one-to-one tutoring. Their expectations from the group were very high, we were to be the leaders in developing this programme; others would follow.

I was impressed with the product knowledge and sales process training, but as soon as the trainers talked about prospecting new business it was clear they were moving out of their comfort zone. Not one of them picked up a telephone to show us how a call should be made, or give us a structure to actually find potential corporate customers.

Coaching followed the classroom training and I had an experienced consultant visit me twice a month to examine progress and to guide me with what he or she thought would be a next good set of actions.

The problem was I was having limited success and the consultant wanted to talk theory.

They understood the sales funnel and had all the statistics about how many calls I should make each day in order to generate the right level of appointments. In fact they set a target of 15 fresh business decision maker contacts per week, which they would check up on during their next visit (a good way to justify their time and you can imagine how this got abused!)

They didn't talk about:

- Who are the right prospects?
- How would I find them?
- What should I say when I call?
- How to deal with the gatekeeper?
- How to gain an appointment?

I felt certain that as and when I made an appointment, that my sales skills would hold up and I could make a sale. I wasn't about to fail as I had too much riding on this position for my livelihood.  What was apparent however, was the approach to small businesses was very hard work and unproductive. I could spend many hours getting through to the Managing Director of a local business only to discover he had no interest in buying our brand and the rest of the fleet was insignificant.

I decided to pick on bigger targets. What was the point in dealing with local business people if it only meant one or two potential sales? I decided to seek out the "Big Cheese".

Within my area of responsibility was the head office of a National house building company and they were growing rapidly. I decided they would have a need for many company cars and their profile fit my product.  After researching their web site I understood a great deal more about their vision and goals and I was able to identify the name and contact details of the Managing Director.

I came up with a plan.

It would take an original approach to even get to speak to this person. I had to have something that was non-threatening and position myself in the right way. (Don't be another salesperson)

My approach was to befriend the gatekeeper, in this case the personal assistant to the MD. I explained that I was new to the local area in terms of corporate car sales and I have no intention of selling to the Company, but to engage her assistance in completing a survey on our brand and the incentive that was available to her superior.

I had arranged an exclusive meal for two at a stylish restaurant in town (I already had a deal with them to minimise the cost) and to offer this up to the Managing Director as a thank you for providing feedback on our new model car.

His part in the deal was for me to present him with the top of the range vehicle to use to drive to the restaurant. The only other caveat was that I would have twenty minutes of his time upon collection of the car to gather his feedback.

It worked delightfully. When I picked up the keys I was directed directly to the MD's office (a nice guy...not a giant after all!). Coffee and pleasantries were exchanged and a quick review of the car. As it turns out he was impressed but not sufficiently enough to change his Jaguar.

The result however was not in making a sale at the top level but the introductions he made to me down the line within his organisation. He introduced me to the fleet buyer and you can imagine his enthusiasm to keep his boss happy. I made many sales at a lower level and price was no longer at the forefront of discussion; it was all about the relationship.

It gets better. As I had made this association at the top level and he appreciated my approach, I started to receive outstanding referrals from his business colleagues.
Life is rich!

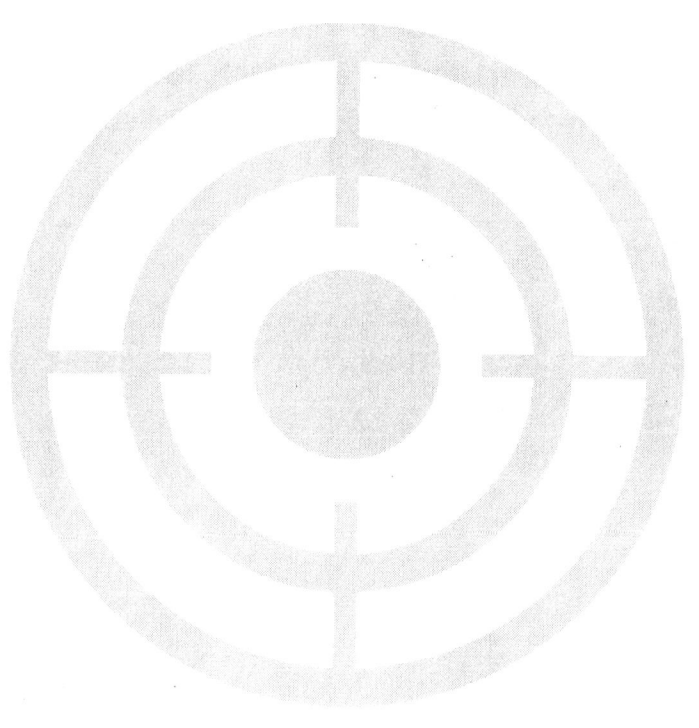

# CONCLUSION

So where are we? What decisions have we made? And what do I hope to achieve from this book? My bit is quite easy. I've had a lifetime of frustrations in making a living through sales and it's taught me a lot. I'm a ongoing learner and I really enjoy looking at what I've done; what worked and what didn't whilst adapting to situations to enable me to be one step ahead. This has provided me with not only a roof over my head, (although sometimes we came close) but a generous living for me and my family.

When I share my experiences with others and show them methods to improve their situation, they are incredibly grateful. I've played a part in the success of many people and gained long-term friends.

I remember a phrase from my Grandma (you remember; the one that was disgruntled with my Grandpa) she said: **_"Don't hide your light under a bushel"_** which is a Geordie phrase meaning; if you've got something good to say... then say it!

My issue is getting my thoughts and experiences out to the world. When you work one-to-one there can be a dramatic impact for clients but I need to share my thoughts "One to Many" and this book is the start of that process.

## What about you?

What will you do as a result of bearing with me through these pages?

Has it had any impact at all? Will you consider changing anything with your approach to sales?

I don't know what you do; you may be in sales for capital contracts or B2B products or you run a market stall or small shop. The fact is...it doesn't matter...because the sales principles are exactly the same.

If you cannot generate leads; you will go out of business!

But the good news is you are "driving the bus". You can decide how many leads you want to deal with. You can decide on the quality of those leads and you can decide whether you want to do business with them or not!

If you control the level of sales activity...You are in control of your business.

I have attempted to keep this book as short as possible, with enough content to inspire and intrigue you. So if you have taken anything away and implemented ideas, then I'm delighted.

I will leave you with a quote from a salesperson that I worked with several years ago. After demonstrating telephone techniques and prospecting customers, he said:

*I just wanted to drop you a quick line and thank you for yesterday. You have changed my opinion and enthusiasm for telephone prospecting and taught me something new, that really works.*

*I will definitely be putting my new found skills into practice more often and hopefully selling more.*

*Once again thank you.*

Remember the telephone is only a piece of plastic. As members of the human race, we have the power to engage.

# CONCLUSION - SUMMARY

- Be different

- Smile and expect a good result

- Prepare, prepare, prepare

- Be alive on the telephone

- Tell your story with conviction

- Know your outcome

- Expect opposition and have your strategy ready

- What's the worst that can happen?

## FINAL POINTS TO CONSIDER:

What is your why?

..........................................................................................................

Who is your audience?

..........................................................................................................

What is the greatest challenge facing your audience?

..........................................................................................................

How are you different?

..........................................................................................................

What problems are you going to Solve?

..........................................................................................................

What difference will it make to your clients?

..........................................................................................................

How easy is it for them to make a decision on your offer/products?

..........................................................................................................

Who are your competitors?

..........................................................................................................

What testimonials can you provide?

..........................................................................................................

How do you view a long term relantionship with you client?

..........................................................................................................

**NOTES:**

Lightning Source UK Ltd.
Milton Keynes UK
UKOW03f1827061216

289344UK00001B/288/P